The Technique of Building Personal Leadership

PROVED WAYS FOR INCREASING THE POWERS OF LEADERSHIP

BY

DONALD A. LAIRD, Ph.D., Sci.D.

WITH THE ASSISTANCE OF

ELEANOR C. LAIRD, A.B. in L.S.

New York   MC GRAW-HILL BOOK COMPANY, INC.   *London*

THE TECHNIQUE OF BUILDING PERSONAL LEADERSHIP

Copyright, 1944, *by the* McGraw-Hill Book Company, Inc.

NINTH PRINTING

Printed in the United States of America

Contents

"I have seen men with fine minds who failed to make their plans effective because they lacked understanding of how to work with people. In our business I should say that this psychological ability and personality mean 75 per cent of the necessary equipment. The ability to get people to work together is of the greatest importance."

—ALFRED P. SLOAN, JR., *Chairman of General Motors Corporation.*

It Can Be Done

Battles are, above all, conflicts of spirit.
Defeat is inevitable from the moment the
hope of conquering fails.

Success Comes

Therefore, not to him who has suffered the least loss, but
✳ to him whose will is strongest ✳
and whose spirit has the finest temper.

Stick-to-itiveness is encouraged by this motto which Philip D. Wagoner, president of Underwood Elliott Fisher Co., gives to all their employees and customers.

1

The personality of the leader

Most people want better jobs—they want to be bosses.

Yet one of every organization's greatest difficulties is to find people who can be leaders. Corporations are ever on the search for people who can lead, and many go to considerable expense to develop leadership in promising employees.

Thousands have been taught successful ways of handling people, but still business and social institutions look for leadership material. Teaching rules for handling people, they have discovered, gives a "mechanical leadership." Something more than knowing the rules for dealing with others is needed.

That needed something which rounds out individual leadership is the personality of the leader. The rise and fall and the rise again of a New England business illustrates this.

Everyone in the small city was proud of the success Old George had made. A local boy, with no special opportunities, he had built up the small factory that made the community. As the plant grew, so did the town.

Everyone was equally sorry that his son, Young George—they called him Junior—was not the leader his father had been. Strangers took over the business a few years after Junior had inherited it. The townspeople were genuinely sorry for Junior and did not like to have strangers come in to boss them and make a profit out of their labors.

Junior's father had done his level best to prepare his son for running the business. He started the boy at the bottom, in the dirtiest corner of the plant. Junior worked there until he convinced everyone he could handle a better job.

As Junior slowly worked his way up to the responsibility of handling others, his father carefully coached him in this art, too.

Old George was what people called a natural leader; he was worshiped by the entire force. Junior could not have had a better example to follow, and Junior was an apt pupil. The young man had great admiration for his father and tried earnestly to be just like him.

When the old man passed on, Junior took over. He was near middle life. The signs were favorable. He knew the business from the ground up. He had a good head. His methods of handling people were those of his father. Many of the old-timers said that it was just like working for Old George when he was about forty years old. Everybody was with Junior.

But in a year a couple of keymen told Junior that they were going to work for a competitor. Young George offered them more salary, but they did not stay. They could give no reason for leaving except that they figured a change might be good for them.

In the shop spoilage and rejections began to increase. Production dropped noticeably. Sales kept up but did not increase as the sales in the industry were increasing. The business was not holding its own.

Then the workers began to grumble, although no two agreed on the reasons for their dissatisfaction. Junior tried to offset this by giving all vacations with pay; they appreciated this, but the grumbling continued. Then they were given insurance and other benefits, but the workers' loyalty continued to skid downward.

In heartbroken disgust, Junior sold out, lock, stock, and barrel. He has now soured on the world and talks vaguely about the revolution. He firmly believes that the workers were arrayed against him. He says they were jealous because he inherited some property. He thinks they were deliberate in slowing down and becoming careless. Poor Junior—he is wrong in all his unpleasant accusations against the world and people in it.

Why couldn't he make a go of handling people? He used the same techniques that his father had proved successful. He was just as ambitious as his father. The trouble was that Junior was a mechanical leader. There was nothing special about him that made others warm up. Junior used the right words and phrases, but he did not have the spirit of the leader.

It was the old founder's spirit behind these phrases for handling people that had made him a natural leader.

Old George had a spirit that would have made him a leader even though he violated all the rules in the book. His son would doubtless still be running the business if Old George had instilled his personality, in addition to the rules, into his disappointed son.

Many corporations, eager to develop their young executives, have helped me accumulate material for instilling this spirit of the leader into the men. We showed charts and statistics of qualities that leaders possess. The men and women were impressed by such precision charts and apparently forgot all about them.

Then we tried rating scales: workers reported on foremen's traits, and superintendents rated their foremen. This got results. It made the men mad. They were, however, less interested in improving their own undesirable traits than in finding out which so-and-so made such an unfavorable report on them.

We tried academic lectures on leadership. The men attended because they knew the company was keeping a record of attendance. Most of them promptly forgot these dissertations.

But we got real results in developing the personalities of natural leaders when we worked through their hearts rather than their heads. Biographies, industrial history, and everyday life were combed to discover dramatic stories that would illuminate one aspect or another of the personality of the natural leader. We searched for stories that would grip our listeners, stories they would not be able to forget, stories in which they would feel they were taking part. People may forget the charts and statistics, but they remember the stories. They may sleep through the learned dissertations or be politely bored, but they eagerly drink in the stories.

Such stories, which drive home the qualities of a natural leader, have done more to build the personality of the leader than any other system we have tried. Here, for instance, are two letters I received in the last mail:

"I don't expect you to remember me, but I'll never forget you and your stories about leadership, especially the one about Uncle Will. Seven weeks ago I was appointed general night foreman. Your stories, directly or indirectly, are the cause of this good fortune. No matter how high I climb, I shall always consider you as the person who made the turning point in my life."

And from a western Canadian city of 10,000: "Your talks on leadership produced marvelous results in our community. For me, they were the direct cause of an increase of salary of $50 a month."

Experience with many organizations has amply proved that this way of presenting the personality of the natural leader does get results. This method is used in this book. Reading it should be no chore, and neither should using the suggestions in your daily life. The stories will carry you naturally on the way to greater leadership.

These stories have been told to many production and sales groups on this continent. Some of them have also been published in the following magazines: *American Business, Better Living, Boston Business, Family Circle, The Rotarian, Supervision, This Week,* and *Your Life.* We are indebted to the editors of these magazines for permission to tell the stories again, in a changed form, in this book.

Always remember the leader does not work with tools and materials—he works with people.

The opposite page may be removed from the book and used as a friendly reminder, in a frame or on your desk, of the vital qualities needed for leadership.

GENERAL QUALITIES OF

A Personality

for Leadership

by DR. DONALD A. LAIRD

PERSONAL MAGNETISM

POISE

SELF-CONFIDENCE

OPTIMISM

TACTFULNESS

PROGRESSIVENESS

INITIATIVE

STICK-TO-ITIVENESS

POWER OVER TIME

2

Personal magnetism that wins people

A group of ambitious management executives attended a conference in the Engineering Societies Building in New York City. Almost all the men were college graduates. They were well dressed, well fed, polished. Each stated his opinions carefully and fluently. The meeting simply reeked of logic. But it was getting nowhere. It needed some magnetism to pull it together.

When it seemed that the conference might break up with nothing accomplished, a shrimp of a man sprang to his feet. He wore poorly fitting clothes, cut in the fashion of a bygone day. The other men seemed amused at his appearance—at first. He began to speak, rapidly and in a high-pitched voice. He seemed excited. He had an accent like a Swedish comedian.

Before he had uttered fifty words the dignified men were listening attentively. Their amusement had disappeared. Soon the little old man had the group in the palm of his hand.

Why? Because he was the first to give off sparks!

The stuffed shirts had irradiated dignity but no sparks.

This dried-up pip-squeak, with his shrill voice and a dialect that could be understood only part of the time, sparkled like the noon sunshine on the flowing blue ripples of a river. He lacked looks, bearing, and good speech, which the others had, but he had a priceless

9

something the others lacked—a magnetic personality.

The little man was Carl Barth, the famous industrial engineer. He electrified the group by his personal magnetism.

This does not mean that he had more iron or electricity in his system. These sparks come from certain habits of acting, certain ways of doing everyday things. The story of a well-known scientist who acquired personal magnetism illustrates the point.

He had about as neutral a personality as one could find. He had neither attracted nor repelled people during his fifty years of life. He was neither plus nor minus —just zero.

For twenty-five of his years he had felt frustrated because he had no sparkle. Though he was in middle life now, and presumably "set in his ways," he, skeptically, began to acquire habits of personal magnetism.

Not in twenty-five days, but in twenty-five hours, the change was apparent. His friends could scarcely believe their eyes. One of his fellow workers remarked, "I never thought such a thing was possible. I had to pinch myself to make sure I was not dreaming."

A few days later his wife attended a Red Cross meeting. One of the local four hundred said to her: "Where have you been hiding your husband all these years! He is the most charming professor on the campus. I have always known he was an intellectual giant, but now I find he is a social giant as well. You must bring him to tea soon."

The scientist had only recently discovered how easy it is to have the habits that electrify others, but his wife did not tell on him. Here are the habits that made him become magnetic.

1. *Be active*

Fiorello La Guardia, congressman, mayor, and citizen of the world, has a magnetic personality. It has helped keep him in important offices for years. His short legs would be a handicap to many men who do not have his magnetism, but they keep La Guardia active, continually on the go.

He wears out his shoes, not his trousers.

Magnetic people are active people. They stand up when they might be sitting down. They move when they might be standing still.

Don't get the idea that these magnetic people were born with something different that makes them active. This activity is very often deliberately assumed. Billy Sunday, for instance, was a quiet fellow, who impressed the members of his family as a bit on the indolent side. But when he was on the platform, when he wanted to lead people, he made himself become active. He was, in a sense, acting. His jumping, gesturing, shouting were part of a deliberate plan to be active. He was not born that way—he made himself that way to help him lead others.

Teddy Roosevelt is another who *made* himself active. Alone, he would be relaxed and easygoing. When visitors came, an instant transformation came over him. He moved with vigor, was intensely active, until the visitor left, whereupon he became a relaxed man. The important point is that he assumed an active manner when he was with people, but we should not overlook the fact that he knew how to let down and conserve energy between times. Had he been active every moment, he might have worn himself out prematurely. Be active when with others, relaxed when alone.

Abraham Lincoln, too, was always alive and in motion when with others. Woodrow Wilson, on the other hand, lacked this asset. It was also lacking in Calvin Coolidge.

A western farm boy, left on his own when he was seven years old, built up one of the largest banking systems in the world. He was A. P. Giannini. His activity was so marked that acquaintances called him Perpetual Motion.

Magnetic women, too, have this asset—activity. They are not languid leaners, striking statuesque poses. They are on the move, alert, almost restless. The trained actress cultivates this characteristic, and she can steal a scene from a more beautiful woman who lacks vigor.

Charlotte Cushman started as an operatic singer. She had a marvelous contralto voice, but when she was barely twenty something happened to her voice. Its promise failed; it became almost second-rate. But this, shall we say, cracked voice did not hamper her progress seriously. She used activity and became an outstanding dramatic actress. No particular beauty, no particular voice—but activity.

"A plain face, but of a noble expression," it was written of her. "Her figure tall and elastic, her gait majestic. Her acting was of the restless type—repose she never attained to, nor seemed to desire. When reproached by a friend for her constant action, she replied that her chief rival was so beautiful of feature that she could well be content to stand still and be gazed at. But it was not so with herself; she must occupy the eye with action and movement, for if she were still, half her influence was lost."

Magnetic people show their activity in their handshakes. They use no "dead-fish" handshake, no polite finger touching. They *shake* one's hand.

They use their hands to gesture when they talk; they do not keep them stuffed in pockets. Teddy Roosevelt used his hands to carve out charts and symbols in the air as he talked. This activity holds interest and helps make ideas clear.

Magnetic persons put steam in their talk. They talk more rapidly than neutral people. Most of us should talk faster than we do, in fact. Open your throttle and speed up your words. Observe the popular radio programs for an object lesson in this; try to repeat the words right after the speaker, and you will find he is talking much faster than is habitual with you. Talk faster.

Magnetic folks keep their voices up at the end of sentences. This keeps listeners in an expectant attitude. Let your voice trail off, and you lose your listeners. Keep it up, ending with some emphasis, and you jerk them to attention, electrifying them.

Magnetic folks also give emphasis to some of their words. They pause a split second—electrifying attention by that pause—and then push out a word with more emphasis than usual. This is one of the secrets of Winston Churchill's powerful magnetism over those who hear him. There is no monotone in his talk; he uses emphasis to make it sound like a military polka.

Try it, yourself, on this simple greeting:

"I'm glad to meet you, Mr. Smith."

Now repeat that greeting, putting the emphasis on the words indicated:

"I'm GLAD to meet you, Mr. SMITH."

What a difference! The same words, but sparks are given off when some emphasis is used. In this era of telephones, where telephone personality is important, the *speed* and *emphasis* and *keeping-voice-up* are prime requisites.

Further, you do not need to be born with a musical voice to have magnetic speech. Teddy Roosevelt had a squeaky voice, and knew it. Mayor La Guardia certainly has no booming baritone. It is not the voice you were born with that determines the magnetism; it's how you use that voice. Make it active, along with the other activity of the magnetic personality.

Being active was the first habit, or group of habits, our reformed scientist watched. He began to talk more rapidly, to gesture a bit, to stand and move, and to move a bit faster. People who appear lazy, or simply easygoing, are not magnetic, though their hearts be of gold.

The scientist had not been lazy, but the poor fellow would stay in one spot so long—especially when it was a comfortable chair—that he seemed loath to move. When he started to keep himself moving, to be active around people, to keep his voice power up, people began to consider him a human dynamo and were magnetized by his new sparks.

2. Be brisk

One of the first habits Theodore Roosevelt formed deliberately, in his boyhood, was to be brisk without being brusque. He had an active handshake, but a brief one. He stopped while the other person was expecting one more vigorous pump, one more squeeze of his fingers.

Teddy left them expectant.

His talk was brisk, too. He would talk actively for a few sentences, then stop in silence and let the other person carry on.

His glance was brisk. A few seconds of intense concentration into the other's eyes, then to their hands, jewelry, chin.

He was brisk at social gatherings, the first to excuse himself from friendly groups.

Again, he left them expectant.

The essence of this habit of briskness is to leave people while they are expecting more. Quit while the quitting is good. Don't wear out the welcome. Clear out before you run down.

When people come to talk with you, this briskness can be used, and without offending. Terminate interviews quickly, gracefully. One executive looks at his watch and then stands up to indicate that it is stopping time.

Another pushes back his desk work and lays down his pipe when someone comes into his office. When the discussion has reached the conclusion, so far as he is concerned, he puts his pipe in his mouth and draws the desk work back to him.

I have been in some private offices where a large, hand-lettered motto behind the executive served to remind the caller to be brief. "Time is precious—don't waste it" one of these read. Another said, "To waste one's own time is foolish—to waste others' is stealing." The caller could not fail to see and understand these admonitions as he looked at the executive. And I can give testimony that they made me be a bit briefer.

Most interviews can be brief. When they are not, the talk is likely to run around in circles, repeating itself to no point. Since many do not realize the value of brisk-ness, the executive has to protect himself by such tricks in order to terminate the interview tactfully and un-obtrusively.

But how do you break away from an interview? Many say they have trouble finding some excuse. No excuse is necessary. Whether you are leaving someone's office, or a private home:

First. Stand up and say: "I simply have to go now!"

Second. Take your things and go!

Don't let anything stop you between the first and second steps. If you are asked why you must go, well, say that Laird told you to—and don't stop; keep right on moving.

When you start to leave, don't stand still; keep mov-ing, and toward the door. Don't talk, either. Smile and keep going right out the door.

Neglect to be brief, and one becomes a bore. When Lord Dufferin arrived late at a luncheon, he apologized to the hostess by explaining that he had been detained by the Earl of Kimberley. Then he whispered: "A wonderful man! It is amazing how much he knows. He knows everything—everything!—all the corners of the earth and all the men in it. He knows everything, except—except when to stop!"

In his early days as toll collector on the canal, John H. Patterson had a small retail coal business as a sideline. He was continually short of money because people were slow to pay for their coal. His business was too small, too insecure, to serve as a basis for bank credit. But he borrowed, solely on his own credit. One morning he went to his banker and said:

"Mr. Phillips, I want to borrow $500 until Friday."

"Write out a check for $500 to Mr. Patterson," the banker instructed a clerk. Then he turned to the embryo businessman. "Let me give you a little advice. If you had not asked for it the way you did, if you had asked me how I felt and how business is, you would not have the money. Always be brief. And another thing, be sure to have the money back on Friday."

Busy businessmen appreciate brevity.

But be careful that you do not become curt in striving for this brevity.

In preparing written reports, brevity should also be nurtured. When a report is inescapably long, boil it down in a few words of summary. Put this summary at the very beginning of the report. Nine times out of ten this summary will be all the boss reads. If there is no summary, he is likely not to read it at all.

Don't pretend you need a lot of words or a long report. That is an admission either that you don't know how to use English or that the report is mostly words and no meat.

The whole story of the creation is told in 400 words in the Bible. The Ten Commandments contain only 297 words. Lincoln's imperishable Gettysburg Address contains only 266 words. Our Declaration of Independence can be typed on three pages.

Yet I have seen a serious report on why an electric fan was needed, and the report contained four charts, two diagrams, and six single-spaced typewritten pages. (The junior executive did *not* get the fan after all that work.)

It was such lack of briefness that led the comedian to observe that Sampson was a piker. Sampson used the jawbone of an ass to slay ten thousand Philistines, while a few million of us kill our chances with the same weapon each day.

Our forlorn scientist had been in the habit of talking and talking. He quickly learned to talk actively for a few moments, then to listen.

It was not easy, at first, for him to break away while conversation was still flowing stimulatingly, but he made himself do it.

He formerly told many long stories, which people thought boresome. Now he tells the same stories in a fourth the time. He tells one and quits. People say that he seems to have developed a sense of humor.

It was a ginger-headed farm-implement salesman who summarized this habit of being brisk: "I get what you mean. Kiss 'em and run!" [1]

[1] For more examples of being brisk see Chapter 2 in my book entitled "The Technique of Handling People."

3. Be cheerful

Only office boys seem to be drawn to funerals (especially on the day the home team is playing in town).

The radio programs with the high ratings are the ones that feature comedy.

And people who have grouches or who let the corners of their mouths turn down are about as magnetic as an old maid at a bachelor party.

Will Rogers endeared himself to the entire world by his cheering face and words. His humor was a cheerful outlook on things others worried about.

His writing was cheerful. His talk was cheerful. He looked cheerful.

Smiling Charlie was the nickname for Charles M. Schwab.

Thomas Lipton's smile and perpetual cheerfulness took him a long way, too.

And remember that toothy grin of Teddy's?

Then there was Max Schling. He landed in this land of opportunity, from his native Austria, and went to work for $4 a week. After two years he had $35 capital, so he went in business for himself. But he had other capital that was worth much more than that $35. He knew flowers and had a talent for arranging them attractively. In addition he had a "sunny disposition," as the newspapers headlined it. Of course, a man who works with flowers might be expected to have a sunny disposition, but he had more sunshine in his smile and voice than any other florist in New York City.

The first day his profit was $1.64. Business grew day

by day, and at the end of the year his $35 had earned him $10,000. Or did his cash capital earn that? How about the capital of his sunny, cheerful personality? At its peak, that smile was bringing in sales for a million dollars' worth of flowers a year.

Royalty, aristocrats, and the Broadway great passed by other florists to call on Sunny Max Schling. They did not get cut-rate prices on their flowers, not by a jugful, but they got some sunshine thrown in with their purchases.

Have you ever noticed bosses' nicknames, especially those used only behind their backs? Many of these uncomplimentary nicknames show that the boss does not use the ingredient of cheerfulness in his dealings with his workers, such names, for instance, as (Gloomy) Gus, Groucho, Snooper, Old Brimstone, Wailing Willie, Scrooge, Bad News Charlie.

I was in a small Georgia city one springlike Saturday. Two legless beggars were seeking alms on the public square. One was whimpering, whining. The other had a mongrel dog, which he fondled as he smiled at the passers-by. I watched from a distance for a half hour. Eight persons gave alms to the smiling man with the dog. Two others gave to both beggars.

People who have personal magnetism must be cheerful. They talk about glad tidings, not calamity. They encourage others, never emphasize discouragement. No matter what obstacles they realize are ahead, they talk and act success, not failure.

Others feel better after a few minutes with such people.

Just as the magnetic person leaves others feeling expectant by his briskness, so does he leave them in elevated moods by his cheerfulness, even when he has to pretend that cheerfulness. And more successful persons than you realize *pretend* they are cheerful.

I have a friend who had enough troubles to make him an ingrown grouch. Bert was seriously concerned about these, to be sure, but his wide circle of friends said they envied him his inborn fortitude. Inborn, nothing!

"I figured," Bert told me with a warm smile, "that it wouldn't help others any if I went around grouching and telling about my troubles. Neither would it do me any good, nor solve the trouble. So why not make them think I'm happy, even if I'm not!"

The scientist we are using as an example had the habit of talking about the minor tragedies of life in a doleful voice. Much of the time he looked as if he had just swallowed a snake.

He sounds much more pleasant now that he keeps his voice power up at the end of sentences. When the voice drops, it gives a doleful impression.

He complained about the aloofness of salespeople, but when he approached them with a smile, he instantly found that they smiled back and gave him interested attention.

There is magnetism in a smile, in every evidence of cheerfulness.

4. Be direct

A few years ago a blind student majored in my courses. Of the two dozen majoring students, he was by all odds the most magnetic and the most popular. He was, in fact, the most magnetic man on the campus. It was not because the students were sorry for Pat, either. He earned the popularity by being active, brisk, and cheerful. So were many other students, but Pat's blindness, strangely enough, helped him to be more direct than any of the others.

Since he could not see those to whom he was talking, he spoke intently in the direction of their voices. He turned his face in that direction. He faced others when he talked to them and did not talk out of the corner of his mouth. Sightless, he spoke more directly to others than most people do. The scientist had the habit of talking to the floor; Pat talked to people. Pat was direct.

The man who looks at the ceiling, out of the window, or at the third vest button is not being direct.

There are sparks given off when one looks intently at another, regardless of which one is doing the talking at the moment. That is what the blind student did, and since his atrophied eyes were hidden behind dark glasses he did not glare people out of countenance.

A man who has specialized in training retail sales clerks tells me that one of the most common errors of beginners is to look at the goods they are displaying. They should look at the customer, talk to the customer.

Superstitious folks aver that there are people who have magnetic eyes. Any eyes are magnetic when they look directly at one. The intently direct eyes of a pet dog, even, have a magnetic effect on its owner. Watch a dog sometime. When its master moves slightly, the dog follows the movement. The dog's eyes remain intently fixed. The master may be reading, giving the dog no apparent notice, but when his eyes do fall upon the dog, there is the animal looking intently at him. Probably that is one reason why many dogs are more magnetic than many people.

The leader has power over others from his direct glance and direct manner. There is a "look in the eye" of the leader. It is not a fierce or a haughty look; it is a direct look. He does not glare (the way Mussolini tried to do) or stare, like a country bumpkin on his first visit to the city. The leader looks intently at others. That intent, direct look establishes contact.

Many advertising managers insist that, in their illustrative advertising, the central figure in the picture should be looking at the reader—directness again, even on the printed page.

"Why did Jones fall for that girl? She is homely and poor—two strikes on them at the start." Well, men do fall for many girls just because the lassies have directness in their glances, as many flirts with wandering smiles know.

And when a girl does have beauty and background, *plus* directness, look out, men! One woman, for instance, wondered what Peggy Upton Archer Hopkins Joyce Morner had that she didn't have. Peggy Joyce, she is usually called; the other names she has won on the field of matrimony. The woman in question saw Peggy Joyce at a night club and watched her, green-eyed with jealousy. She thinks she discovered one of Miss Joyce's secrets of power over others.

When Miss Joyce and her escort were seated, the magnetic Peggy turned and looked carefully at the other tables. She satisfied her curiosity about the people who were there, whom they were with, and what they were wearing. Then she turned to her escort and never took her eyes off him for the rest of the evening.

You can't be magnetic by talking to the ceiling or looking at the floor.

5. Be exciting

Have you ever noticed that effeminate men rarely become leaders?

On the other hand, it has been said of many outstanding men that they are leaders of men and followers of women.

A clean interest in the opposite sex is a mark of normal emotional development. Perhaps a fourth of adults lack this, and while they may be brilliant and accomplished, they usually lack magnetism and leadership. Others, though having a normal interest in the opposite gender, spend their lives trying to suppress this perfectly natural interest; they become the stiff, cramped, nonmagnetic people.

One unfortunate aspect of this is that some people of admittedly loose behavior have their looseness condoned or overlooked because it is one of the things that reflects their magnetism.

Magnetic Benjamin Franklin, for instance, was a life-long flirt. In the heat of youth he became the father of a couple of illegitimate children. He did not conceal these steps from grace, and to this day the old families in Philadelphia are not reconciled to that terrible man Franklin. In his old age Franklin was still making playful love to bishops' daughters, on the one hand, and to French countesses on the other. In all frankness, he was a despicable old rogue, but he was magnetic. The pity is that he could have been magnetic without being as extreme as he was in his affairs with the opposite sex.

Philip Armour was kicked out of elementary school near Oneida, N. Y., for taking afternoons off from school . . . in company with schoolgirls. That kick started him toward becoming the great meat packer in Chicago, and that kick was caused by his interest in the opposite sex.

John Charles Frémont, western explorer of the gold-rush days and a candidate for the presidency, was also expelled from school—Charleston College—for his love affairs.

The most magnetic man of revolutionary days, Alexander Hamilton, himself probably an illegitimate child, could organize affairs of government but could not keep his own heart affairs from causing severe concern. Washington put up with Hamilton's indiscretions because Hamilton was indispensable.

Charlie Schwab always had a soft eye for the girls. In Loretto they still talk about his love-making at the early age of seventeen.

Magnetic Andrew Carnegie, although he was almost an old man before he married, was always aflutter for feminine society. Merry Andrew, the boys called the Scot who was magnetizing people and piling up a fortune. He eyed all the ladies with best regard.

Although John D. Rockefeller was no hail fellow well met, not a mixer or joiner, his stern Baptist personality still carried considerable magnetism. There was something impelling about the young man who was to become an oil baron. He kept his eyes glued to his ledgers but also looked often at a well-turned ankle. He fell in love in his adolescence and wanted to get married right away, but Melinda Miller's mother broke that up quickly; she said the young fellow would never amount to much. Those who claim he was in love with money only do not know his life history. He lived to the ripe old age of ninety but was never too old to yearn.

The eyes of magnetic Cyrus H. K. Curtis, the newsboy from Maine who built the Curtis Publishing Company, sparkled their brightest when looking at the fair sex. At sixteen, he was working in a dry-goods store in Portland, receiving $3 a week. The Portland girls and women literally flocked to buy yard goods and prints from the handsome young man who looked at them with eyes that saw more than a customer.

Long before the movie producers discovered this magnetism, in both men and women, Alexander T. Stewart was making it pay in his department store in New York. Stewart, an Irish immigrant, started in a hole in the wall but soon owned the largest department store of the time. He had fancied Irish colleens, and he also fancied many of his customers. He discovered that the customers he fancied bought the most goods and were the quickest to return to buy more. So his policy was to employ the handsomest men he could find. If the men openly flirted with his customers, Stewart never complained. The "nice young men" in Stewart's establishment became the talk of the town, and sales soared.

It is unfortunate, of course, that moral turpitude and social radiance seem to go together. But one can still have the radiance without the turpitude. Watch that.

In developing from infancy to maturity the normal person passes through three distinct stages. From birth until around six or eight years of age is a period primarily of self-interest.

This early period gradually changes into one in which the interest is extended to others of the same sex. This is the time, from about eight until around fourteen, when boys are interested more in boys than in girls. The boys have their gangs and seem to think girls are a nuisance, to put it mildly. The girls, too, have their own play groups and do not show much interest in boys, other than to say they are terrible, and the girls mean it—then. This is the period of interest in the same sex that makes possible the Boys Scouts, Girl Scouts, and similar organizations.

After high-school age, it is difficult to hold these groups together. A spontaneous change in interests is the cause. The boys are extending their horizons and becoming interested in the girls they thought were nuisances only a couple of years before. The girls, for their part, undergo a corresponding shift in interests and begin to feel that boys are pretty important, after all. From high-school age on, that is the normal development.

But a few men and women, as previously noted, seem to stop before the final stage of maturity. Those men who are really woman haters belong in this underdeveloped stage. Of course, the perverts of both sexes have not reached the final stage of development. These under-developed folks may be hard workers and achieve considerable by sheer effort. They may have a fair success in leading people, largely by ordering them around or by having groups of yes men. They may be active, brisk, cheerful, and direct but still not give off sparks because they lack full emotional development toward the opposite sex.[1]

[1] For the application of these facts in saleswork see the chapter "The customer desires to purchase romance," in my book entitled "What Makes People Buy."

Normally, this interest in the opposite sex does not fade with age. Justice Oliver Wendell Holmes, of the Supreme Court, was a magnetic personality. One afternoon, when he was more than eighty years old, he was walking with a companion. An unusually attractive woman passed. The old justice turned to watch the woman after she had passed. He touched his companion's arm and said: "Ah! If I were only a young fellow of seventy again!"

The scientist had been conducting himself as though he had not yet been told the facts of life. As a prudent married man, he was so cautious that the womenfolk thought he must hate women.

The men believed he had ice water in his veins.

He was almost shocked to learn that one of the most important ingredients in personal magnetism is a strong, yet idealistic and controlled, interest in the opposite sex. He had been pretending to ignore women, when he should have shown his interest in them by many little gallantries.

By trying to conceal his natural interest in women, he had become artificial, stiff, aloof. It had made him inhibited in many ways.

At last he started to be himself. He did not begin to flirt, chase around, or become the least bit vulgar. But he did notice women's clothes, for instance, and compliment them. He no longer hid in the attic when women visited his wife. He gallantly greeted them at the door, looked directly into their eyes for a moment, and smiled.

He now stops to chat for a moment with women acquaintances when he meets them, in place of the previous hat tipping and bowing as he went on his way.

He is still just as moral and circumspect as ever—and likely will always be that way—but he has verified the fact that there is a strong biological element in personal magnetism.

Women take to him now because they realize that he enjoys their company, because he flatters them by his gallant ways.

The men have come to believe that the scientist is, after all, just as human as the rest of them. And they respect him for being "clean" and free from vulgarities.

Some people are afraid that it is dynamite to be exciting. It is not in the case of normal people. It is a basic factor in all personality development, as well as in electrifying others.

6. *Be fearless*

The scientist had always been extremely cautious about offending people. He had his convictions, to be sure, but he kept them to himself for fear he might cross someone. Not for love or money would he have done the unpopular thing. He went with the stream.

Such safe playing is apt to win contempt. Such folks are called the Mr. Milquetoasts. They are spineless, wishy-washy. Like a rubber stamp, they lack character and individuality.

The scientist's character and accomplishments were without blemish, yet people looked down on him instead of respecting him. His playing-safe policy was revealed in every word and gesture. He had his convictions but was so pussyfooting about them that people guessed the opposite. He was a yes man.

But he studied both President Roosevelts, Lincoln, Franklin, Carnegie. He discovered that anyone who had personal magnetism had a mind of his own. Such folks stand by their convictions, even when they are not popular beliefs. The natural leader has the gumption to scrap, if necessary, for what he thinks is right. He "speaks out in meeting" against injustice, graft, obsolete methods, blunders by the high and mighty.

John D. Rockefeller, Jr., has this quality of fearlessness. When he was a relatively young man, for example, there was a violent strike in a Colorado mine that his family controlled. The burly miners were threatening physical harm to their bosses.

When the turmoil was at its height, young Rockefeller boarded a train for Colorado. He was going to beard the lion in its den, as well as find out, from firsthand observation, what conditions actually were.

"He'll be torn limb from limb by those infuriated miners," thousands of people thought.

But Rockefeller, serene and calm, went directly to the miners. He slept in their hovels, ate with them in their kitchens. Against advice, he had no bodyguards to protect him. Fearlessness!

This quality shows itself not just by sticking one's chin out when there is trouble around. It is reflected in the tone of voice, firmness of glance and lips. It gains respect for the leader—and wins followers.

A veteran paratrooper was sitting at an adjoining table in the dining car. He was a private first class. His face was bronzed and firm. Three naval petty officers sat down at the table with him. The sailors had seen no active service; the paratrooper had. The sailors asked him dozens of questions, and he replied to each in a clipped firm but pleasant voice.

The sailors finished first, and as they left the table, each extended his hand to the unknown paratrooper and wished him good luck. He held the sailors in the palm of his hand because he seemed to ooze fearlessness from every pore.

In words, actions, and thoughts, the leader must be fearless. People, animals, and even vegetable life respond to the person who shows no fear.

I was helping my uncle on his small farm. Thistles had sprung up in the hayfield, and he put me to work clearing them out. I approached the first one tenderly, then let out a yelp of pain as its nettles stung my hand. Although it was a blistering hot day, I set up a cry for leather gloves to handle the thistles.

"It's easy, if you know how," my uncle said. "Look, like this. Grab hold firmly, as if you meant business. That crushes the prickers. *Never pat a thistle.*"

Some time later I was sent to a neighbor's farm on an errand. As I neared the farmhouse, the dusk was gathering rapidly. I didn't relish walking back in the dark. Then I heard the neighbor's vicious watchdogs raising a noise at my approach. How I hated to complete the errand!

But it was too late to turn back, because the dogs were approaching me now, and there was not a friendly sign in the pack.

Then I remembered my uncle's words: *Never pat a thistle.*

"Lie down! Get into the barn, you whelps," I shouted at the dogs with all the mock courage I could put into my voice. I picked a stone from the roadside and threw it at the pack. They did what I had planned doing myself a few moments earlier. They ran the other way.

"Hello, kid," their master said as I went to his back porch. "Didn't think anybody was comin'. What's the matter with them dawgs of mine? Mebbe I've been feeding them too well!"

The lesson of those two experiences has been useful for me many times in dealing with people. Perhaps you feel no more bravery than I really felt, but show courage anyway.

Lloyd George, the Welsh boy who became British Prime Minister and virtual dictator during the First World War, got his magnetic start in life from his fearlessness in speaking frankly. As a young lawyer of twenty-one, David Lloyd George talked to the magistrates with a candor that shocked the experienced barristers. He did not call a spade a spade; he called it a dirty symbol of unfairness and prejudice. Yet the magistrates did not hold him in contempt of court, though he might well have been.

At one trial, for example, Lloyd George said the court had no jurisdiction in the matter.

"That," replied the magistrate grandiloquently, "must be decided by a higher court."

"And in a perfectly just and unbiased court," young Lloyd George added.

The magistrate stared open-eyed at this fearlessness. "A more insulting remark I have never heard during my experience on the bench," he said.

"And a truer remark was never made in any court of justice," the Welshman added.

Lloyd George was not afraid of the overbearing magistrate. The young barrister felt he was right and stood by his guns. The biased magistrate withdrew from the case, and the upstart's courage avoided a contempt charge.

Henry Ford has the courage of his convictions—that's fearlessness. He fought the Selden patent monopoly. This fearlessness attracted John Wanamaker, who took the agency for Ford automobiles way back in 1903. Wanamaker joined in the fight against what he, too, considered an unholy patent monopoly.

During the bloody Homestead labor riots, Henry Clay Frick may have been unwise in some respects, but he apparently remained fearless. Although his life had been threatened repeatedly, he continued his ways and his work as usual, refusing the bodyguard suggested for him. Newspapers spread this story, and, of course, some unsympathetic individuals read it—and wondered.

One of these readers was an intelligent young man who had convictions, but not much courage. Alexander Berkman paced nervously outside the building in which Frick's office was located. Young Berkman, an anarchist, was jumpy, fingering a concealed pistol with one hand, a homemade dagger with the other. He wanted to, yet he lacked courage.

In a nervous sweat he dashed into the building and rushed up the single flight of stairs and into Frick's open office. Berkman took three shots at close range. He was so afraid that one went wild. As Frick crumpled to the floor, Berkman jumped on him and inflicted several deep wounds with his dagger.

By this time the commotion had attracted workers from the other offices. They rushed into the bloody, smoky office. One grabbed the assailant's revolver and turned it to shoot Berkman.

Frick, weakened from loss of blood, saw this. "Don't shoot!" he whispered. "Leave it to the law. But raise my head so I can look at him."

Frick's head was raised. He noticed that one of Berkman's cheeks was puffy.

"See what he has in his mouth," Frick said.

They found a packet of fulminate of mercury. "I was going to blow this whole room, and myself, all to hell," the anarchist blubbered.

In all the excitement, Frick was the coolest person in the room. He helped probe for the two bullets and completed the unfinished work on his desk before getting into the ambulance.

Do you wonder that men were drawn to him?

Don't overlook moral courage in connection with fearlessness. Teddy Roosevelt had physical fearlessness. A Wild West character, making fun of Teddy's eyeglasses, picked a fight and drew a brace of guns on the effete easterner. The bullets hit in the ceiling as Teddy landed on the bad man with such force that the troublemaker was laid out cold. A few years later, low political rivals hired "Stubby" Collins, an underworld strong-arm man, to beat up Teddy in the Delavan House in Albany. A few moments after Stubby accosted his "victim," the accoster was being revived by his friends.

But keep an eye on Teddy's moral courage, too. That is as important in leadership as physical courage. It takes both brands to make real leadership.

He would fight for an ideal, for what he believed was right, with just as much force as he would struggle to save his own life. There was the time, for instance, when he was indignant over some of the things being attempted by some factions of organized labor. Now a scheming politician is supposed to humor labor along, to be sure of their vote. But Roosevelt won more votes than he lost by his moral courage—he stood on a platform in front of an audience of thousands, shook an angry finger in the face of Samuel Gompers, head of the American Federation of Labor, and denounced him roundly.

Imagine the electric nature of that occasion. There were sparks aplenty!

No wishy-washy person would have the courage to do that. No yes man could do it. It took fearlessness, of which Roosevelt had a magnetic share.

(Since this chapter was first written, the scientist discussed has been appointed Dean of the Graduate School of a great Middle-Western university.)

For PERSONAL MAGNETISM that WINS PEOPLE

Be active	Be brisk
Be cheerful	Be direct
Be exciting	Be fearless

3

Poise that makes one master of situations

Can you take a reprimand without blowing up?

Can you take a turndown without being visibly discouraged?

Can you laugh with the others when the joke is on you?

Can you keep your spirits up when things go wrong?

Can you speak in public without being noticeably ill at ease?

Can you keep cool in emergencies?

The natural leader answers all these with a confident *yes.*

It is poise that makes one master of such situations. The natural leader is often a person who has *deliberately acquired* this poise. Consider public speaking, for instance. The name of Daniel Webster, stanch defender of our Constitution and golden-tongued orator, is at the top of the list. As a young man, no one suspected he might some day become the greatest orator of his time. In fact, he failed miserably the first time he tried to speak in public. Here is what Webster himself said about this embarrassing boyhood experience:

"I could not speak before the school. Many a piece did I commit to memory and rehearse in my room over and over again, but when the day came, and the schoolmaster called my name, and I saw all eyes turned upon me, I could not raise myself from my seat. When the occasion was over I went home and wept bitter tears of mortification."

His famous poise in later life was a deliberate accomplishment.

Adolf Hitler's lack of poise is shown by his mannerism of patting his stomach. And Generalissimo Francisco Franco, a cat's paw for Hitler, keeps wiping his forehead with a handkerchief. Look around you in any conference and you will see many such mannerisms and gestures, which reflect a lack of poise.

No one expects all high-school seniors to have perfect poise, especially when they are sitting self-consciously, in brand-new clothes, before their proud parents and friends, waiting to receive their diplomas.

But they should have some poise. I was recently astounded to see such a group completely lacking in poise. As I look back to that evening, I regret I did not talk to them about poise, for they surely needed that more than the graduation message I gave them.

And the adults! They were worse than the youngsters. The principal was a cuff shooter. His cuffs were all right, but every few minutes he would adjust first one, then the other. He played with his sleeves so much I expected to see him pull a rabbit out of them.

The matronly member of the school board may merely have been laced up too tightly, but she acted like a confirmed girdle adjuster.

The treasurer of the school board was a ceiling looker. He sneaked a look at the audience now and then, but apparently he didn't have the courage to face them so he kept studying the ceiling.

The minister who delivered the invocation was a pulpit patter. He draped his long hands over the front edge of the pulpit and emphasized his words by patting it. His hands were perspiring, the varnish was sticky, and most of his pats smacked noisily, like a cow pulling her foot out of the mud.

One of the seniors, an attractive lad with freckles, was a nose rubber. He rubbed it with the back of his left hand, incessantly. His nose turned up a bit, and I wondered if he had rubbed it into a tilt.

Another boy kept scratching one spot on his head.

Another was an ear puller.

The prettiest girl in the front row was a handkerchief tugger. She kept rolling her handkerchief into a rope and then having a one-person tug of war.

A blonde with a tantalizing smile was a foot tapper. Perhaps she was a jitterbug at heart. She sounded like a one-person telegraph set.

The two really poised people were the plump girl and the gangling president of the school board.

The pudgy girl was astonished to hear that she had won the D.A.R. prize, but she came forward to receive it with amazing grace. She was perfectly poised and beamed a winsome smile as she was given a crisp new ten-dollar bill. (The boy who won the science prize was so unpoised that he tripped over his own feet when he returned to his seat.)

The president of the school board was a self-made man. Even his clothes looked self-made. He was one of the tallest and thinnest men I have ever seen.

He was an onion broker. His language was awkward. He may have known his onions, but he was not well acquainted with the English grammar.

But during the few minutes he spoke all these peculiarities seemed to disappear. He was at ease, calm, graceful in his gaunt way, well poised.

He had the least schooling of anyone on that platform —and the most poise!

Lack of poise is due to negligence, neglect of simple little habits. Here is what happened to one man who was giving himself the wrong start. He was beginning to fidget so much that people were uncomfortable in his presence. He was getting so ill at ease that he was justly worrying about himself and his future.

He was a brilliant young attorney, handicapped by a lack of poise. When things became difficult or when it looked as if a decision might go against him, he lost all poise.

Opposition lawyers had been quick to notice this, and capitalized on it. They made a point of annoying him until his nervous fidgeting turned into a complete loss of control.

He seemed destined for only a mediocre career, but he was wise enough to realize that he should do something to improve his poise. The five things he did for himself are easily remembered: each begins with the letter T.

1. *Think about the other person*

Those sweet young graduates were thinking about themselves.

The attorney was thinking too much about what winning a case meant to him, instead of what the opposition attorneys were scheming.

Young George—Junior—was thinking too much about

himself. The worse things went with him in the factory, the more he thought about himself.

We gain poise when we become less conscious of ourselves and more interested in others.

Our young attorney, for instance, pretended an interest in others at court by counting the wrinkles on another attorney's face during dull hearings. Previously he had tapped the table nervously, but, by thinking about another person, he remained more composed.

He looked at the neckties the jurymen were wearing, and each juror was flattered to see the attorney looking intently at him. Formerly he had had the practice of tugging away at his own necktie until the knot was finger-stained.

Thinking about others, even in these petty ways, helped him to forget himself, to be more poised, and to put his brilliant brain to work without the handicap of self-conscious fidgeting.

The natural leader has power over others because they can sense that he is thinking about them.

From homesteader to the King's representative as Lieutenant Governor of one of the great provinces of western Canada sums the career of His Worship Archibald McNabb. He is by far the most popular governor of all the provinces, for he thinks about other people. This gave him poise when the King and Queen of England visited his province.

There is nothing "high society" about Archie, as everyone respectfully calls him, and people were afraid Archie would commit a grievous social blunder when he sat beside the King at the dinner in Regina.

"Don't you speak," his advisers told him, "except when the King speaks to you."

But Archie couldn't stand much silence. Anyway, he was interested in the other person. Finally Archie tugged the King's sleeve slyly, and whispered:

"Wish you'd brought the kids along."

His social advisers may not have approved, but George the Sixth did. Archie was thinking about the interests of the other person.

It is not because I am a Scotsman living in penny-pinching New England that I make the following suggestion. It is based on sound psychology.

When you are in a restaurant with someone, do you occasionally have a struggle over being allowed to pay the check? Don't struggle. Accede to the other person's wishes. Express your appreciation for his kindness, and drop the matter. Both of you will likely lose poise if there is a struggle for the chance to do the favor. Follow the same practice when offering to carry a parcel for another. If the answer is "No," accept that as final and talk about something else in which your companion is interested.

Those much despised yes men get farther than they would otherwise because they have the knack of thinking about the other person.

I imagine one might be a little ill at ease when meeting the President of the United States. Helen was, but she didn't shake hands with him after all. Her husband was president of a management association that was holding a convention in Washington. Arrangements had been made for the delegates to visit the White House and shake hands with President Warren G. Harding.

Helen was so expectant she could scarcely sleep the night before. She went to the beauty shop for mud packs, a permanent wave, and everything, in preparation for meeting the President himself. She had a new dress for the occasion, the most expensive she had ever owned.

If she did not make the best possible impression, it was not going to be her fault. She put everything she had, and all she could wheedle from her husband, into it.

Then the big moment came. Just inside the door, there stood President Harding. Beside him was her husband, presenting each delegate and each wife to the President. Helen took a quick look at herself in a mirror to make certain everything was just right. As the line moved toward the door she tripped slightly on the rug.

A secret service man helped her right herself and encouraged her by saying: "That's all right. Many people get very nervous."

She scarcely had time to straighten her girdle after the stumble when it was her turn to be presented to the President of the United States.

Flustered, she seized her husband's hand, shook it briefly, and hurried on. She passed by Warren Harding.

She was thinking mostly of her appearance, not of the other person.

2. *Touch a talisman*

The publisher of one of our foremost newspapers was recently hauled before a government board. He knew the attorneys were out to get him and would do everything possible to make him blow up on the witness stand.

He was determined to keep his poise under the severe grilling he would receive, so he used a talisman. He is not a superstitious person and has no belief in magical charms, but he knew this talisman would help him keep poised.

The talisman was nothing more than a small piece of paper. On it he had written: "Keep cool. Don't be smart. Smile."

He carried this in his side coat pocket. While on the witness stand he kept his hand in this pocket, fingering the talisman that reminded him to keep poised.

When he was on the verge of snapping back with a smart answer, the paper reminded him not to be foolish.

It kept him smiling, much to the irritation of those who cross-examined him viciously, trying to get him mixed up.

This talisman kept him calm, and his calmness so exasperated his opposition that they were the ones who blew up.

A secret prop of this sort helps give confidence. It takes the place of a trusted adviser to whisper encouragement and sensible advice.

The secret prop our young attorney selected was a photostat of a complimentary note that had been sent to him by a prominent attorney. He had the copy mounted between two transparent sheets and carried it in his pocket. He seldom looked at it—the friendly feel was reminder enough.

Young Sam Houston was a lively, high-spirited lad, who caused his widowed mother more trouble than her other eight children combined. Sam had just turned twenty when he was aroused by the War of 1812. When a recruiting demonstration took place in his small Tennessee town, Sam stepped up and took a silver dollar from the drumhead. He was in the regular army by that token, but, since he was under age, he needed permission from his mother.

She handed him a gun, saying, "My son, take this musket and never disgrace it: for remember, I had rather all my sons should fill one grave than that one of them should turn his back to save his life."

Then she slipped a plain gold ring on his finger. Inside this ring was engraved a single word. That ring was his talisman for fifty years. The one word in contact with his flesh guided him through a lifetime of danger and leadership where others faltered.

It brought him back to little Maryville, in a year, wounded, the outstanding local hero of the war.

As a result of that talisman President Andrew Jackson esteemed Sam above all other men he knew.

It caused Houston to resign as Governor of Tennessee rather than say a word to besmirch a woman's reputation.

It led to conduct which gave Sam Houston, above all others, the confidence of the Indian tribes of the South and Southwest.

That talisman gave him force to lead a wavering mongrel army to defeat a trained army twice its size and liberate Texas. Twice he was president of the Republic of Texas. He, more than any other, brought Texas into the Union at last.

It was not until his death that any man knew the command of that talisman he had used for half a century. Then his wife slipped the ring from his lifeless finger and held it to the light so that his children, too,

could see the word that had led Samuel Houston steadfastly through trials to victories. The word was
"Honor."

A talisman, however, does have its limitations. When
Sir Walter Raleigh was a schoolboy, for instance, he
was plagued by a boy who always excelled him at reci-
tations. Young Raleigh soon found how to cripple his
rival. He noticed that each time the boy stood to recite,
he fingered one of the brass buttons on his jacket. At the
first opportunity, Raleigh surreptitiously cut off the
"magic" button.

The next time Raleigh's opponent stood up to recite,
his fingers automatically reached for the button, but the
button was gone. The star pupil fidgeted, lost his poise,
and at last young Raleigh saw his rival go down in defeat.

Perhaps the best talisman one can have is a diploma
or certificate from a college, night school, or correspondence school. A certificate of membership in a professional society can also be a helpful talisman. More
people would have a talisman of this sort but for the
unpleasant fact that one has to work to get it.

A row of books—recent books, dealing with one's
business or profession—also help poise by serving as
talismans. Put them on your desk or on a shelf in plain
sight. And . . . don't forget to read them! That helps
poise most; it gives you assurance that you have something extra in your head.

Sometimes the talisman is not so secret but just as
effective. Swagger sticks, for example, are issued to army
officers so that they will have something to keep their

hands busy. They hold onto the sticks and do not tug awkwardly at their pockets. A walking stick gives many men poise in the same way, but be careful not to be caught with one in the factory.

Some executives use a brief case as a substitute for a swagger stick; others use a watch charm.

A western plant superintendent told me that he always carries too much money to be safe, but, since he keeps his hand on his wallet during a conference, this adds both to his poise and to his self-confidence, as we shall see in the next chapter.

3. *Think twice before talking*

John D. Rockefeller was not much of a talker, but he did a lot of thinking before he opened his mouth. He took more abuse, both to his face and behind his back, than almost any other man of his day, yet it did not fluster him.

Jay Gould was another who listened more than he talked. He was downright secretive. During the gold market panic on Black Friday, 1873, a panic that Jay Gould himself manipulated, he was the only poised person on the exchange. He simply didn't talk more than was absolutely necessary.

The poised person has often done his thinking a day, or a week, before he talks. He has planned for possible emergencies and what to do in them. When the emergency strikes, he remains poised because he has prepared for it.

A good word can be said for the "canned" sales talk on this score. The salesman who uses this is prepared to say the best thing when an objection or unusual situation arises, without losing his self-composure.

When folk are angry, flustered, or lose their poise, they let their tongues run away with their heads. Under strain, they may say things they regret later, or they may merely become incoherent.

The cure? Talk deliberately. Think twice before speaking when under strain.

The person who talks deliberately thinks ahead of his words. His mind keeps a phrase or two ahead of his tongue and lips.

The brain should be used before the tongue.

Collect your thoughts—the right thoughts—before speaking. Pause while talking, if necessary, to collect more. (And don't stall in the pauses by growling "er-r-r" or "well-l-l.") The thoughtful talker seldom lacks poise.

It is the old admonition to think twice before speaking.

4. *Take slow, deep breaths*

When people lose poise they breathe quickly. Their breaths are shallow. This does not mean that people lose poise because they have run out of wind, however.

It does mean that deliberately watching breathing, when in a tight situation, will help to keep poise. An amusing application of this was told me by a man who had three times asked the boss for a raise. Each time he had run out of breath and been scarcely able to talk. The fourth time he forced himself to take slow, deep breaths and, for once, was in control of himself and the situation. He got the raise.

It is almost impossible to be flustered when we deliberately breathe slowly and deeply. The young attorney mentioned above calls this, jokingly, his air-cooled system of breathing, since it helps him keep as cool as a cucumber.

Elbert H. Gary, of the Steel Trust, was in many tight situations where it would have been easy to lose poise. That he was sorely tried at times was revealed to his intimates when the top of his balding head turned red. But Judge Gary always thought twice, breathed deeply, and kept his poise. Thus he did not lose control of his temper and the situation.

The famous gossip columnist of ancient Greece and Rome, Plutarch, tells about a prominent Roman who had an unfortunate tendency to lose his poise. As a cure for this, the old Roman had a slave accompany him and blow a low note on a pitch pipe whenever he showed signs of losing poise. Whereupon he would take a couple of deep breaths and lower the tone of his voice to the pitch of the pipe.

When your voice begins to rise, poise starts to leave. Take two deep breaths and lower your voice.

Often, in discussion, we imitate the other person, and when his voice begins to rise ours follows up the scale in pursuit. But when the other person's voice climbs, that is the time, of all times, when we should keep ours in a low, poised register. Many moderate discussions have ended in heated arguments from this inclination for voices to be raised. Let the other fellow talk louder and louder; it is evidence you are winning.

A word should be said about the desirability of having a quiet room for conferences. If the room is noisy, voices have to be raised for ordinary conversation, and the situation is dangerous for poise right at the outset.

You salesmen, get in a quiet location with your customers.

You foremen, get the firm to build you a quiet office, where you can talk over grievances, wage adjustments, and other ticklish problems without need for raised voices.

And all of you, when your voice starts to climb, take two deep breaths and haul it into a lower register.

5. Talk your troubles over

There is usually a feeling of uncertainty behind a lack of poise. Concealed worries, troubles, and little anxieties generate this lack of poise.

The first four aids to greater poise help alleviate the symptoms but are not likely to remove the cause.

The cause, that feeling of uncertainty, needs to be removed.

Married people are usually more poised than the unmarried, the separated, or the divorced. Married folk can talk their troubles over with each other, except, unfortunately, the troubles they cause each other. They can get their nondomestic troubles off their chests at home.

This is another reason why marriage should be based upon more than infatuation. It is sound psychological advice not to marry a person, regardless of the attraction, unless there is a lift in one's spirit after talking some real troubles over with him.

Concealed disappointments, suppressed worries, and restrained tantrums create a backwash that sweeps poise out to sea. When these anxieties are confided in a friend or loved one, the troubles are shared; the burden is made lighter because they are no longer hidden or repressed. The repression causes worse effects than the troubles or disappointments.

This is good medicine for many personality troubles, this talking things over with someone in whom you have confidence. Usually an older, a more experienced, or a better educated person is the one with whom to talk.

Concealed troubles are the natural enemy of poise.

Some people are able to talk their troubles over with themselves and then dismiss the trouble. A young office worker, for instance, was disappointed because his work did not seem to be appreciated. He was on the verge of complaining to his employer about it, and, in preparation for this ordeal, he wrote out notes, for his own benefit, analyzing his troubles, the bad policies of the company, and his own assets.

It made a long list and surely gave him two thoughts before speaking. He was amazed to find that he felt much better after preparing this argument to confound the boss. If things were as he had outlined in preparing the brief, they would soon work out all right. He went back to his work with renewed zest, added poise.

And when he became president of the American Bank Note Co., Daniel E. Woodhull still followed this trick—he wrote his troubles out for himself.

He called it his safety valve.

For POISE to make you MASTER OF
        SITUATIONS

Think about the other person
Touch a talisman
Think twice before talking
Take slow, deep breaths
Talk your troubles over

4

Self-confidence in dealing with others

John Wanamaker went into business for himself on his life savings. In other words, he started out on a shoestring. It took some close figuring and planning, but he embarked on expansions and installed innovations in merchandising that others, who had adequate capital, would not risk. He got through all right, but there were many tight squeezes. He would have been wiped out on several occasions but for his self-confidence and his ability to inspire the same confidence in his associates.

"Such was our faith in him," one of his associates said, "that we never thought of possible failure. Whatever the stress, we were always sure that, in some way, he would find the way through. Looking back, we sometimes wonder. But at the time we never doubted. We leaned upon him, his cheerfulness and courage, with the confidence of children in a parent who had never failed them."

Wanamaker handled people to bring out their confidence. One time, in a rearrangement of departments, he changed a buyer's work. The buyer was afraid he couldn't make good in the new department.

"I've just bought a new house and have the mortgage to pay," he told Mr. Wanamaker.

"I can protect your mortgage."

"No. I'll try to work it out myself," the buyer said, starting for the door dejectedly.

"Look here," Mr. Wanamaker shot at him, "I have more confidence in you than you have in yourself."

That challenging comment from the boss struck home. The buyer, in a strange department, became one of the successes of the organization. Confidence gave him the go-ahead attitude he needed.

Like the buyer, many find they can develop self-confidence. It is not as born in one as the pessimists like to pretend. But in developing self-confidence, it is possible to get too much of a good thing. Self-confidence then becomes arrogance, foolhardiness, a liability. Consider, for instance, this true story.

Three young physicians opened shop the same fall in a small western college town. "Which of the young chaps will make the best doctor?" everyone asked.

One of these young physicians we can honestly call Dr. Timid. He had the best located, most modern office. He knew medicine and minor surgery, but he was not quite certain of himself. He kept to himself. He took considerable time to think before prescribing for a patient. He hesitated to forecast the outcome of a case.

At the other extreme was the doctor we can call Dr. Blow. He had graduated from the weakest medical college but was self-confident to an extreme. He knew the answers to all questions. Cigar sticking jauntily upward, he could tell—and without being asked—how to get more mileage from an automobile, who should be elected mayor, how marvelously he had set a broken shoulder. He could tell his patients what was wrong before they recited all their symptoms. His pills were sure cures, so he implied. He joined every organization in town and tried to run each of them.

Then there was Dr. Ordinary. He was about midway between the extremes of Drs. Timid and Blow. He was confident and sure of himself but unassuming. He was not a braggart, like Dr. Blow, or a church mouse, like Dr. Timid.

Six years later this was their status.

Dr. Ordinary was the success. He had finished payments on a rambling old mansion that he had bought for a song and converted, at some expense, into a private hospital. Patients flocked to him.

Dr. Timid had finally saved enough to make the down payment on a house and had just moved his office into it. He did not need much space for his patients.

Dr. Blow was still frantically dunning patients, to scrape together enough money each month for payments on the showy house he had bought when he first settled in the town, intent on becoming a big shot. The house was much bigger than his business.

The same story might be told about almost any business. Dr. Ordinary forged ahead, became the medical leader, because his confident manner inspired confidence.

Dr. Timid obviously lacked it. So did Dr. Blow, but he tried to conceal his lack of self-confidence by being bold and overly confident. This assumed air of confidence did not evoke the confidence of others. It annoyed them. It usually does.

Dr. Blow is too deeply set in his overcompensation, as it is called, to become an ordinary, self-confident person. He will continue through life a bluffer and braggart.

On the other hand, Dr. Timid can do wonders toward gaining a natural self-confidence. Timidity is always hopeful; overconfidence is well-nigh hopeless. Here are the things that Dr. Timid, and the many others who need greater natural confidence, should do to acquire the confidence the leader must have.

1. *Put long trousers on childhood memories*

How grown-up I felt when grandfather took me into Patterson's store on the square in Indiana and bought my first pair of long trousers. I can still remember the herringbone pattern in those long brown legs, which seemed to change my whole attitude toward life. I was grown-up at last. Grandfather had said so, and that proved it.

But it takes more than the clothes of an adult to give one the personality of an adult. That is why many folk need to put long trousers on their memories—to grow up, by putting many of their childhood experiences into an adult perspective. Neurotics, for instance, retain a childish outlook.

Low self-confidence is usually the result of lingering memories of failure, or unfavorable comparisons with others, which were made in childhood. People who need more self-confidence are often letting themselves be dominated by childhood discouragements. We have to put long trousers on these memories, get them into an adult perspective, and then they will quite likely become amusing rather than handicapping.

An industrial executive had not made the progress his training and ability warranted. The vice-president told him frankly that he needed to impress others as being more confident.

He had heard about putting long trousers on his childhood memories, and tried it. At the age of five he had
recited a verse at a Sunday-school program. On one
word he lisped, and the audience laughed. The laughter
upset him so that he forgot the rest of the verse and left
the platform in tears.

The mental poison from that childhood reaction had
lingered for a quarter century. It lowered his self-confidence, until he raised it with the viewpoint of an adult.
Now he can laugh about that lisp, but for years he was
always timid when talking for fear of lisping.

Inadequate self-confidence almost always grows from
some such childhood experience. Here are some childhood memories, for instance, which people have recently uncovered and on which they have put long
trousers and thereafter gone on their ways with increased self-confidence.

"From mother we always received criticism. She com-
pared us with other children so that we looked smaller
in our own eyes. I know now that she did this to stimulate us to do work she could be proud of, but it had the
opposite effect on me. I had never thought before of the
implication this had, but I sure feel more confident after
recalling this."

Another: "Now I realize where I got this feeling of
numb helplessness. When I was about six, mother left
me and a younger sister to take care of the baby. When
mother returned, my sister told how much she had done
for the baby, implying I had done nothing. That evening some people came in to visit, and I heard mother
tell them how wonderful my sister had been that afternoon, and how much more dependable she was. I 'went

numb' then. That is the same helpless feeling which has been holding me back in my contacts with people."

And another: "I haven't liked to talk about this, but it was when we moved from the farm into a college town that my low self-confidence got started. The city children made fun of my homemade clothes, my need of a haircut, and so on. It has secretly rankled me ever since, but I have, foolishly, I now realize, tried to hide this. I have worked hard to beat the city-born youngsters and have succeeded. But I have needed much more self-confidence."

Those stories are typical. Embarrassments, shames, or discouraging comparisons in childhood linger on unless they are put in an adult perspective.

Each of those stories is, after all, a bit amusing. When each one who had the experience could look back on it and relate it with appreciation of the fact that it "was 'way back when I was a youngster," then his self-confidence picked up.

It is good for mental health in general and self-confidence in particular for you to be able to tell about the things that annoyed you in childhood, but tell about them with a twinkle in your eye. You are grown-up now, you remember.

Don't be ashamed of having been a damned fool years ago. Tell about it frankly. Laugh about it. You are still a fool, however, if you maintain a childish attitude toward childhood's storms and stresses. It is difficult to forget these episodes of bygone years, but you can—yes, must—look upon them as impressions that were strong just because you had a childish point of view. Take a grown-up's view of the experience and have a chuckle for yourself.

Childish boners are more than excusable. Adult sensitiveness about them, however, is another thing. It is a thing that robs one of self-confidence.

One day a friend offered to help Themistocles improve his memory. "Ah! Rather teach me the art of forgetting," the great Greek replied, "for I often remember what I would not, and cannot forget what I would."

He had the general idea, but in recent years psychoanalysts have discovered that the attitude one has toward one's memories is as important as the memories themselves. The important thing is not to forget the childish things, but to look back on them with the mind of a man.

Maybe your childhood was not happy; there are many bumps and unpleasant memories from every childhood. How differently you would have taken those experiences if you had known as much then as you do now, at least if you have the attitude of a grownup.

That is what we mean by putting long trousers on your childhood memories.

You wept or sulked about it then. Now smile and chuckle at them.

2. Secretly belittle others

Underestimating your own ability will rob you of the nerve to start.

All too often your own ability is good enough, but you overestimate the ability of the other person. That condition results in lowered self-confidence.

Dr. Blow did not underestimate his own abilities. He

had an inflated notion of them. As the high-school principal described Dr. Blow confidentially to some friends, the overly confident physician made him think of the way Euripides described that mythical beast, the Minotaur:

A mingled form, prodigious to behold;
Half bull, half man!

Dr. Timid belittled himself and magnified others. That is what is done by most people who lack self-confidence. They need to reverse the telescope, to belittle the other person, but *secretly*.

Richard was assigned to interview corporation presidents on a money-raising campaign. Here was a chance to get some recognition and good experience. But he broke into a cold sweat and lost his nerve just outside the office doors. He made weak-kneed calls on ten men, lost about ten pounds doing it, and raised practically nothing.

His wise old counselor told him to belittle others secretly as an aid to keep up self-confidence.

"Do you mean," Richard asked, "that I should say to myself on entering their offices, 'Who the hell are you?'" Well, that was the general idea.

Armed with this formula he returned to the first corporation president. Going up in the elevator he began to belittle. As he stepped off the elevator he muttered to himself, "Who the hell was he, anyway!"

That seemed so ridiculous that he smiled to himself. And that smile was a million-dollar smile of confidence. It won a contribution, and he kept getting contributions from the other big shots.

Turn the telescope around so that you seem bigger, others smaller.

Dr. Blow belittled people, but to their faces. Do it secretly and smile at your secret nerve in doing it.

A young immigrant was the butt of many jokes in a bakery. He was learning the new language and made many amusing blunders. Young Michael Pupin felt that the other workers were his superiors and manifested a properly humble respect toward them. But inwardly, secretly, he knew he was their superior in some ways. He studied popular-science magazines and science articles in the Sunday newspapers, and the others knew nothing about science. As young Michael kept up his study of science, his self-confidence gained by leaps and bounds. He became assistant engineer in the cracker factory, then a millionaire inventor of electrical devices.

Quite often the grass looks greener in the other fellow's pasture. Salesmen think that a competitor's product may have some superiority, after all. Industrial executives may imagine that another corporation has more opportunity.

Such thoughts belittle the wrong thing. Don't belittle your present opportunities; make the best of them.

Do belittle a competitive product or firm, not publicly, however, but *secretly*.

The only time Harvey Firestone failed was when he was a traveling salesman for a relative who manufactured a hand lotion and some patent medicines. Young Firestone used the Wild Rose Lotion himself when his hands were chapped, and he knew it was a good product, but he had no faith at all in the patent medicines.

He sold lots of the lotion, but he couldn't get store-keepers to buy any of the medicines. He secretly belittled those medicines, and he could not sell them because of this lack of confidence.

Belittle the right things—and do it secretly. When it is done openly, as Dr. Blow did, others lose confidence in you.

3. Put your best foot forward

This is the other side of belittling others: build yourself up in your own estimation. Watch your best foot.

Marjorie's story is typical of many who need more self-confidence. Her husband had a good job, and they went with a better crowd than she had been used to. She had not traveled, was not a college graduate, did not have prominent relatives. She was watching the things she did not have or could not do, and her attention on the wrong foot was burdening her down.

She wanted to move to a small town, wanted her husband to take a less important job. But her husband realized that that would not solve her difficulty, that what she needed was to change her perception of herself. So he suggested that she list the things she did well.

She played the piano, for instance, far better than anyone in her crowd. She excelled in raising flowers. There were many other little accomplishments that she listed. She was amazed at the length of the list.

"Why," she exclaimed with a faint blush, "it almost seems like bragging. I just never realized this. Guess I've been looking at the hole rather than the doughnut."

She tucked the list in the bosom of her dress, like a talisman, where she carried it for several weeks. She added items to the list—a splendid sign, for it indicated she was now thinking of herself in a positive way.

Dr. Blow kept his eye on his good foot, too. He made his mistake when he told others about his goodness.

Watch your best foot, but do it as *secretly* as you belittle others.

If you don't have a best foot, develop one. Get some special accomplishment. Read. Study. Read the trade magazines in your field. Buy new technical books in your field. Read the front page of a newspaper daily.

Get acquainted with the merchandise you handle. Learn more about its uses, how it is made, where the ingredients come from.

Talk with some old-timers to learn the history of your locality, of your firm.

Self-education does wonders. It gives confidence by developing some best feet to put forward.

A metal-trades firm has an unusual method of picking executives. The general manager will not approve a new executive until he has played poker with him. His theory is that a man who can put on a confident front when he has a poor hand is a man who can put his best foot forward even when he has no best foot. There is one objection to this, however. The general manager may be collecting a bunch of executives who bluff at self-confidence, like Dr. Blow.

Athletic coaches like to start the season with opponents that will not be too difficult to defeat. These easy victories at the outset of the season keep the team from losing confidence. Prize fighters are brought up carefully through a series of matches of increasing difficulty to keep ring confidence. Hitler started the Second World War by first invading small countries that would be easily conquered, thus bolstering up the confidence of his armies and of the home front for the harder fighting to come. These are all tactics to help self-confidence by putting the best foot forward.

One of the most successful public-speaking coaches follows the same strategy. Young executives enter his class flushed a deep red with anxiety because they have to stand on their feet and talk. The master teacher builds their self-confidence by easy stages. The first gives them something in which success is certain: he has each one stand and tell his name and address. Now that was easy, wasn't it? And you have a good voice quality.

Then each takes his turn at standing for one minute—timed by a watch—and telling something about his work. Pshaw! That was easy, too. Thus the pupils get some confidence in their ability to stand up and talk.

Try that when you are starting something. Do the part you are sure you can do and keep up confidence for the rest of the job. When breaking in new workers, also, follow the same strategy for building self-confidence.

As the Chinese proverb says, a trip of a thousand miles starts with a single step.

The shoes on your feet should not be overlooked, however. They play an interesting part in self-confidence, putting your best foot forward.

Did you ever examine a pair of army shoes? They have hard leather heels. When a soldier walks down the street he can hear himself.

But listen to an Australian fighting man come down the street. He makes much more noise. There are tiny steel plates on the heels and toes of his shoes. Each step is resonant, sounds firm. It is a little trick to give the men an increased feeling of confidence as they walk.

I recommend leather heels for all bosses, not only to help them walk confidently, but also to eliminate any suspicion on the part of employees that the boss goes prowling around quietly, trying to catch the force loafing.

4. Put money in the bank regularly

Dr. Blow tried to bolster his lagging self-confidence by living in a bigger house and driving more expensive cars than he could afford. Dr. Ordinary saved systematically. No one knew how much Dr. Ordinary was saving; that was his secret. But everyone knew how much Dr. Blow was spending.

Self-confidence comes, however, not from what the world knows about us, but from the secrets of superiority we ourselves have.

Money itself is not an important thing, but it gives a feeling of security, of getting ahead, that is vital for self-confidence.

Recently I was talking with a college graduate who needs more self-confidence badly. His pay has been practically doubled in the past year, yet he is broke and more in debt than ever. He spends his money right and left in a frantic effort to get more self-confidence by impressing others. He needs, however, to impress himself. His spending and debts put him further behind in self-confidence. The more involved he gets, naturally the less security he feels.

It isn't what people get or spend but what they save that helps self-confidence. As the balance grows, so does the feeling of security.

Accident and sickness insurance helps, and so does life insurance. I like to have owners of life insurance look at the table of cash values of their policies on each birthday. The growing increase in their equity boosts self-confidence a notch each year.

Buying a home of one's own gives another boost, especially if the place is modest enough so that insurance and savings will not suffer. Go on a cash basis as soon as possible—today!

John D. Rockefeller, Sr., was a saver even as a young-ster. By the time he was nine he had saved enough to be in business for himself.

"A young man may have many friends," Sir Thomas Lipton said, "but he will find none so steadfast, so constant, so ready to respond to his wants, so capable of pushing him ahead, as a little book with the name of a bank on the cover. Saving creates independence, it gives a young man standing, it fills him with vigor, it stimulates him with the proper energy; in fact, it brings to him the best part of any success—happiness and contentment."

And that energetic boy from Pittsfield, Mass., who built one of the greatest fortunes in the world—Marshall Field—said: "Never give a note. Never buy a share of stock on margin. Never borrow. Work always on a cash basis. Buy for cash and sell on short time."

John H. Patterson, who built up the National Cash

Register Company from an idea that other men had failed to put across, kept his eye on the ball, his business. He made no investments; his earnings all went into his business. He did not have other irons in the fire to distract his thinking, to undermine his confidence when one of them slumped. This paid him, not only in self-confidence, but also in a half million dollars a year for many years.

Another man who kept his eye on the ball, with no outside investments, is Henry Ford.

A horseradish peddler who became one of our largest food manufacturers, H. J. Heinz, built his business from scratch by saving and putting every penny back into the business. No speculation, even when he could afford the risk; the money went into new products, more advertising, expanded plant facilities.

Cyrus H. K. Curtis, builder of *The Saturday Evening Post*, *Ladies' Home Journal*, and *Country Gentleman*, put money into only those things in which he was directly and actively interested. "Too many men have slipped up there," he said. "They make money in a business they understand, and then invest it in some business which they do not understand. A shoemaker should stick to his last." As Mr. Curtis earned extra money—and there were many times when he could scarcely meet his pay roll—he stuck to his last and used it to strengthen his enterprises.

The Scotch bobbin boy, Andrew Carnegie, practiced the same. "Put your eggs in *one* basket," he said, "and then watch that basket." Early in life he bought some shares of railroad stock. But from then on he put money only into his business or into the bank.

"Nothing tells in the long run like good judgment,"

Carnegie said, "and sound judgment cannot remain with the man who is disturbed by the ups and downs of the stock exchanges. He jumps at conclusions which he should reach by reason. His mind is upon the stock quotations and not upon the points that require calm thought."

Thomas A. Edison's first profitable invention was a stock ticker, yet he himself never speculated. When he sold an invention to Western Union, he asked them to pay him in installments over a seventeen-year period, so that he would not need to think about what to do with the money. He made the same arrangement with them a few years later, in disposing of another invention. He was wise not to have something to divert his thinking.

The tall engineer who built General Motors Corporation, Alfred P. Sloan, Jr., wrote: ". . . my philosophy on the subject of savings grows out of my own experience. I have seen General Motors go from $85 a share to $7, but I never sold a single share. Speculation never had any attraction for me. Other than a few professional operators, who really gets ahead by stock-market trading?"

Horace Greeley rose from a debt-ridden New England family to become founder and owner of the largest and most influential paper of his time, the *New York Herald*. Adviser of presidents and bankers, he wrote:

"For my own part—and I speak from sad experience— I would rather be a convict in State prison, a slave in a rice-swamp, than to pass through life under the harrow of a debt. Let no young man misjudge himself unfortunate, or truly poor, so long as he has the use of his limbs and faculties and is free from debt. Hunger, cold, rags, hard work, contempt, suspicion, unjust reproach, are disagreeable; but debt is infinitely worse than them all."

There are two good places to pour your money: into your business and into your head—read, take courses, attend meetings.

For SELF-CONFIDENCE to CONTROL OTHERS

Put long trousers on childhood memories
Secretly belittle others
Put your best foot forward
Put money in the bank regularly

To feel confident, act confident.

5

How moods can help our work

Well, that's that. Now we have hit bottom and there is no way for us to go but up."

This was the calm comment of a business friend who had just received word that his best customer, for whom he spent more than three million dollars a year, was transferring his business to a competitor.

Only a few weeks earlier I had seen this same man storming and stewing because his firm had lost a customer who spent only twenty thousand a year. Then he was sure that the lost business would ruin him.

Why was he such a poor loser one day, such a good one another, and when he really had bad news? It was because the news of the small loss came on one of his bad days, when he was moody. The serious loss came on one of his good days.

We all have our ups and downs, some of us worse than others. Many persons are handicapped by these, but some have learned how they can actually use these ups and downs to give them greater leadership.

An acquaintance came to me about her blues. She had a bad dose of them at the time and claimed she always had them. I knew of some home movies her husband had made when she was having a hilarious time at a picnic. When she saw the movies again, they did not make her feel happier but they did convince her that she was not always in the blues.

Some persons have dug out their diaries and read back over the entries to see the regular rise and fall of their spirits over a period of years. Some have even made charts from these entries.

One person could not do this because he kept a record only when he was feeling on top of the world. This proved especially useful, however, for he now rereads the entries when he gets in a downcast mood, and the memories thus aroused help make his bad days more bearable.

An unusually successful salesman uses a somewhat similar trick. He has photostatic copies made of his best sales orders and carries these in his wallet. When the blues get him, he looks at these for objective encouragement; they keep his sales up.

A Philadelphia sales manager had noticed shifts in his moods but had not noted their clocklike regularity. "I have days," he said, "when my men all seem to deserve a raise. A couple of weeks later, I want to fire the lot of them.

"When I am up," he continued, "I think my wife is beautiful, and I'm bursting with pride over my youngsters. I get lots of ideas. I want to be with folks. Then, suddenly, a few days later I'm a changed man. I am down. My wife looks a sight to me, I worry about the kids, I want to be left by myself, and I find fault with everything I have done."

He might have added that when he is "up" he eats more, walks and talks faster, wakes up early, feels peppy, makes wildcat investments, laughs off criticism and blunders. This is the time to ask him for a raise, a loan, or a new fur coat.

When he is "down" his appetite is poor, he talks and moves slowly, is constipated for a few days, can't get enough sleep. In this mood, he returns articles he has bought, takes patent medicines, criticizes everything— himself in particular. He loses interest in the opposite sex. This is the time to leave him alone, to praise him, and beat it.

Moods like these come and go with almost the regularity of the calendar. The average person takes about four weeks to go from one crest of optimism to the next. He passes through the slough of pessimism about midway between. Some people have shorter cycles, taking only two weeks to go through one, while others have long-drawn-out ones, lasting six months.

Abraham Lincoln had a long cycle, which went to extremes. He was in a down cycle when he left his bride waiting at the altar the first time his wedding date was set. It took him several weeks to get over this bad spell, although most of us recover in a day or two. Lincoln was also in a downswing when he delivered his imperishable Gettysburg Address; that is why he felt it was a complete failure. Such a deep funk possessed him on his inauguration day that detectives were assigned to guard him against possible suicide.

These upswings and downswings of mood are perfectly natural, pestiferous as they may be at times. They do not imply insanity. It is dangerous, however, for us to worry about the moods or not to know how to *put them to work*.

The shift from optimism to pessimism is usually so

gradual that most people do not notice the change. They do not realize the change until they discover themselves in the middle of a dark mood. Then, too, there is a natural inclination to give more attention to the blue days and forget the tiptop ones.

The tiptop days have their drawbacks, especially for executives. It is then that people get into debt, make risky investments, turn out a lot of half-baked ideas, start more things than they can finish.

The bad days have their advantages. They give a contrast that makes the upswing seem more enjoyable, the way olives make other food taste better by contrast. Judgment is more on the conservative and safe side, and people watch their health on bad days.

What causes these changes in mood? They are not related to the moon, menstruation, blood pressure, or any other cycles yet discovered. Maybe the ductless glands have something to do with these moods, but this has not yet been proved.

What makes the downswings worse? Psychoanalysts have found that the depression of the bad days is often due to a person's feeling of hostility toward others, his bothered conscience, or a feeling that others do not like him.

Our low moods are not caused by bad luck or failures. They seem to start spontaneously. It is not because others criticize us, but because we are, at those times, our own worst critics.

There are some important rules for handling others, or ourselves, during the downswing. We have to humor people then. Criticism only makes them worse; they are

A mirror reflects

A leader originates

A surly salesperson has surly customers.

A grouchy worker has a grouchy boss, if the boss lacks real leadership.

This is because of the human tendency to reflect the attitude or mood of the person we are facing.

The natural leader must be superhuman in this respect. He must not reflect the moods of those around him. He must be superior to these casual influences. The real leader adopts for himself a mood that others will reflect.

When the real leader is in the presence of someone with an undesirable mood, the leader says silently to himself: "Well, look how he is trying to lead me astray. But I'll be superior to him. I'll adopt for myself a more favorable, a constructive mood. I'll set up a better attitude and maintain it until he is following me."

The leader must, in such ways, be superior to his environment.

He adopts the attitudes that are desirable.

He maintains those attitudes through hell and high water.

Call him an actor if you will, but he remains an originator, not a reflector.

already criticizing themselves too much for their own good. It is wise policy to wait until they are out of the low mood before censuring.

People need praise more than anything else, unless perhaps affection, when they are in the downcast mood.

We should avoid important decisions at both extremes of the mood swings. At the one extreme we are too optimistic and at the other too pessimistic to use good judgment.

A widow in Chicago, left with only a large house, had to convert it into a rooming house to make a living. She has been unusually successful by not making important decisions at either extreme of the swing. She first plans remodeling or redecorations, for instance, when she is at the top; she plans as though expense were not a consideration. She is careful not to put her plans into action, however, until she has gone through a downswing, during which the plans are trimmed to fit her budget. The result is the bright decorative plan of an optimistic mood and the low cost of a realistic, pessimistic mood.

A top-notch advertising executive applies the same procedure in his work on a new campaign. After weeks of toying with various possibilities, he waits to start action when he is in the upswing. Then he works with furious speed, yet easily, on the comprehensive plan. This work is laid aside, to be resumed in about ten days, when he is starting into his downswing. He rips the work apart, directing his surging self-criticism against his plan and copy. Only the soundly justified parts remain.

In the "lucid interval," as he calls it, between the

downswing and the crest, he patches together what he tore apart, and, behold! there is a finished advertising campaign that is inspired, yet soundly based. He has made himself and his clients wealthy by thus tempering his brain storms of optimism with the severe criticism of his blue periods. He would be another fellow full of bright ideas that did not work, if he did not temper them by the tearing apart in his downswings.

When a quick decision of importance is necessary, a conference of several executives is wise. Some of them will be in the optimistic phase, some in the pessimistic, and their average decision is likely to be sound. Associates thus are a good balance wheel against blunders due to moods. This is something one-man concerns lack.

Some take to drinking during their downswings. This may give some temporary relief by drugging the blues, but it makes the next spell all the worse from the self-criticism the drinking causes. It pays to ride out the storms of pessimism; alcohol is no ballast for them.

When in the downcast mood we incline to keep to ourselves. But we should force ourselves to be with others. No pampering allowed!

We feel tired, without having worked, when in the downswing. The salesman thinks he should sit in an air-conditioned movie rather than make calls. The executive thinks he needs to relax in his favorite chair at the club. But they need work, not rest. During the downswing, we should work our hardest.

(For some of the special problems of mood cycles in women see my book entitled, "The Psychology of Supervising the Working Woman.")

To PUT YOUR MOODS TO WORK

Work harder than ever
Make no important decisions
Be with people
Pretend you like people

6

Optimism that begets enthusiasm

The cheerful spirits of a young stable boy caught the attention of Andrew Carnegie.

"Why don't you come to work with me?" Carnegie asked him. "You're the kind of fellow I need in my business."

And so Charlie Schwab was launched on his fabulous career in steel. His good-spirited optimism got him the job and made him one of the master businessmen of his time. It enabled him to sell the elder J. P. Morgan the idea of combining small steel companies to form a giant. Older men had been unable to sell this idea to the financier, but smiling, optimistic Charlie Schwab did it.

The same optimism led Schwab to live beyond his means—and he had a million-dollar-a-year salary. He died insolvent.

His story, thus briefly told, shows the strengths and the weaknesses of optimism. It is needed to influence others, to breed enthusiasm. But it may also lead one into reckless investments or unsound decisions.

Schwab was not perpetually optimistic and cheerful. He had his bad days, like the rest of us. But the dark days were not the ones that gave him his characteristic attitude and manner. He had the priceless faculty of seeming happy, whether he was or not. We'll learn more about this ability shortly.

An optimistic, cheerful attitude is required to get things done, to handle others so that they expend their fullest efforts in the work. Here is the story of Smiling Billy, quoted from an advertisement of the Jones & Lamson Machine Co.

Sure and there are those who'd punch the nose of the man who wouldn't lift one to Billy, tonight—in a dignified fight, of course.

For we've turned back the timeclock to March 7, 1903, when Smiling Billy had a hand in the destiny of a great American industry. . . . He fought a battle with a giant turbine, while history hung in the balance.

He was a shop foreman in one of the early plants of General Electric. His company had pioneered research in turbine engineering, and had staked its reputation on the plans of the first commercial steam turbine generator. It was to be a gigantic machine, and the Commonwealth Edison Company of Chicago had courageously designed their entire new Fiske Street generating station around the plans for this unborn behemoth. . . . The date they had set for the official test was March 7, 1903.

By February, the turbine was still months from completion. A meeting of foremen was called. "Who among our general foremen is 100 per cent qualified to complete the building of the turbine *on time?*" they were asked. A single name had the vote of every man there.

The story of Billy's battle with the turbine is a minor classic of one man's knowledge of machinery, tools and men. Around him lay thousands of unfinished parts. Ahead of him lay the task of assembling a machine as big as a two-story house and as delicate as a lady's watch—that could shatter itself to pieces from a microscopic error in tolerance.

He won. On March 7, less than three weeks from taking over, Smiling Billy waved a grimy hand, and the first big turbine generator began to whine a brand new song of power.

History is made that way.

The men did not vote for Gloomy Gus, or Bull-of-the-Woods, or Pickle-puss Pete to get that rush job through on schedule. They picked a man with smiling optimism. The leader must pick optimism for himself, must seem optimistic even when it is a complete bluff.

Many who seem to be born optimists do their full share of bluffing themselves, and others, with an assumed optimistic enthusiasm.

In a round-table discussion with some industrial executives, someone questioned that statement. "Look at Frank," he said. "If he isn't naturally optimistic all the time I'll eat my hat."

We asked Frank.

"Sure, I have my bad days," Frank said cheerfully. "There used to be times when I hated to look at a person, I was so busy thinking over my petty gripes. But I figured that was getting me nowhere except the booby-hatch. Why crab to others when I'm in the dumps! No one else is interested, and I don't feel any better for it myself. So I began to put on an act when I felt low. That's when I kid most with the fellows and raise Ned. It keeps me from feeling sorry for myself."

1. *Act optimistically*

That is the way to start generating a cheerful feeling through thick and thin. It is essential in leading people.

Marshall Field followed this rule. While Chicago was still smoldering from the great fire of 1871, businessmen along State Street held an open-air conference to decide what to do with the ruins of their stores. They were pessimistic. All thought Chicago was done for, except one, Marshall Field, and he was just getting a start when the fire all but wiped out his business.

He pointed to the smoking ruins of his store, pretended optimism, and told the discouraged group, "On that same location I will build the world's greatest store."

George Westinghouse faced not fire, but the panic of 1907. His business was just getting started, too, and he made a bluff at optimism, and the bluff made him optimistic. That is what usually happens.

His company had gone into the hands of receivers. Many of his associates were disgruntled, ready to quit. They were in the grip of pessimism. But Westinghouse put up a bold front of optimism. He talked about his new ideas for turbines and other devices that would make money for the firm. His pretended spirit of optimism spread, and more than a half million dollars was raised, right within the plant, to keep the company going and prevent liquidation. Think of that whenever you see a Westinghouse trade-mark or when you feel down in the mouth.

Remember the disastrous San Francisco fire of 1906? At that time the bank that young Giannini had started was a year and a half old. Here is how he optimistically and realistically reacted to what might have been the end of his business, as reported by the newspapers:

"After walking for miles through the maze of desolation he reached his bank about noon. The advancing flames were only a block away. He hastily commandeered two wagons. On one he loaded his money and securities. On the other he stacked a supply of banking forms and stationery.

"Where would he take his valuable cargo? Oakland was across the way, with a jagged wall of flames between; to reach the Presidio stronghold would take many miles of travel through a district where pandemonium reigned. He decided to take his precious loads home, which seemed safe, and the treasure was buried there.

"While the ruins of his bank were smoldering, he wrote a circular letter to all his depositors, offering to lend to all who wanted to rebuild. Hundreds took advantage of his offer.

"He set up a temporary desk on the docks, while the fires still burned, the first banker to reestablish his business."

Not only quick action but also optimism is shown by this dramatic incident. Giannini acted optimistically. He always did.

Acting optimistically, as we shall learn later, is half the battle in getting things done successfully. During the War between the States, for instance, Commodore Dupont was telling his superior why he had been unsuccessful in the attack on the monitors at Fort Sumter.

After summing up all the obstacles, the Commodore said: "I did not expect to succeed."

"That is the very reason you did not succeed," Admiral David Farragut replied.

For landing a job, for keeping up one's own morale, acting optimistically is a lift that is hard to beat. An acquaintance of mine had a splendid job as an art director. He had two small children and was awaiting the third. He had just built a delightful house. The future looked rosy, until an unexpected shift in advertising accounts left him without a job. Concern over the payments on his house and the education of his children helped Old Man Gloom get a hold on him. He tried to get work, but in his pessimistic frame of mind, he made such a poor presentation of himself that he got nothing but polite turndowns.

He was going downhill steadily, and his wife was worried about him. He was told about Westinghouse, about Field. Surely he, too, could bluff himself into apparent optimism.

He bought a new suit from an expensive tailor. Dressed in this, he went to New York City on the Pullman, not the bus. His pretense helped revive his optimism, infected those whom he interviewed about work.

He got a job and became a much better art director because he now acts optimistically and he gets enthusiasm from others.

We can't be pessimistic when we act optimistically.

2. Smile—actually laugh

A laugh, or a smile, helps displace a feeling of anxiety. It has a power over other people, too.

Sir Thomas Lipton was often called the world's greatest optimist. Perhaps he was. His optimism played a big part in the development of his business from a small basement neighborhood grocery store to a world-wide chain of stores, plantations, and packing houses. He refused to be gloomy and went through life with an infectious smile and good humor.

He never could win the yacht pennant, try as he did for many years, but he took each defeat so smilingly that the international committee at last awarded him a cup for being a good loser!

His smile won more than loving cups. It won customers in a volume that would make even a Scotsman optimistic about the future.

"In the opening weeks of my store," he said, "I noticed that a smile and a joke were generally well received by the customers, and I also noted that good-humored people spend more freely than those with frowns on their faces."

H. J. Heinz, of 57 Varieties fame and fortune, knew the value of a smile in keeping both customer and worker optimistic. He laughed readily himself. He wanted his employees to smile, so he did unusual things to bring this lesson home to them.

There was one otherwise capable young man, for instance, who seemed unable to smile. H.J. made him assistant to a man with a rich smile.

"Your smile will draw customers," he said, "while the new chap can do the work."

At the end of a week the man with the smile received a raise. Shortly the serious young man asked why he had not received a raise, since he was doing the same work.

"I can afford to pay extra for the other fellow's smile," Mr. Heinz told him. "It is worth something to have someone who smiles."

It is worth a lot to the person himself, also, more than can be counted in cash. A famous Chicago psychiatrist makes his patients tell a funny story at the opening of each therapeutic interview. It is a part of the treatment to make the mentally ailing laugh.

A popular suspicion about smiling has been confirmed by research by Dr. George R. Thornton of Purdue University. He found that others judge a smiling person to be more kindly and honest than one who is not smiling.

I worked for a time with a man who had the greatest smile I have ever seen, even a better smile than Schwab's. He had smiled so much, in fact, that the corners of his mouth had been stretched out of shape. There is an unusual story behind his smile.

He was getting a great start as a professional athlete when he pulled a tendon. He was out of athletics for keeps. At thirty he had to start a new career. Finally he landed in saleswork, but his commissions wouldn't feed a chicken.

The uncertainty over his future, his dwindling resources, all naturally made his pessimistic moods more ingrowing. The worse he felt, the less he sold, and the less he sold, the worse he felt. He was progressing backward.

His sales manager had a heart-to-heart talk with him. Put a smile on that doleful face was his advice.

The salesman tried to smile but produced only a sickly grin. He tried smiling at the bathroom mirror for fifteen minutes every morning but got only that same anemic, unnatural smile, until he discovered that he could bring a warming smile if he first thought of some pleasant things. As soon as he tried to feel friendly, then the good smile came.

The secret was not to try to smile but to feel friendly and let the smile come of its own accord. This little thing changed his life, revolutionized his fortunes.

For more than twenty years now he has been using that exercise every morning. Before he gets out of bed he turns on the friendly feeling, and the smile follows. He keeps smiling while shaving and dressing, and the smile stays the rest of the day.

I have walked down the street in strange cities with him and seen total strangers look a little friendlier as they saw his smiling face. I have seen professional men grant him unusual favors, although he was totally unknown to them. And it always seemed to me that waitresses brought him much larger pieces of pie than I got from them.

It takes a rarely skilled actor to imitate a smile, but anyone can produce a real smile by first feeling friendly.

Never ask for an order, never issue an order, never ask for a favor, never try to influence others in any way, unless you first feel friendly and smile a little.

3. *Swap hostility for affection*

Have you ever watched two dogs meet for the first time, listened to their muffled growls of hostility, wondered if they were going to tear each other to pieces? Sad to admit, too many people have the same hostile attitude toward others. They may not growl or snarl, but they do show a similar hostility by making secret, unfavorable observations of each other's clothes, face, language.

It is hostility of this sort that causes pessimism. Psychoanalysts have shown that a smoldering feeling of hostility crops out as pessimism, a spell of the blues. Optimism is elusive until we learn to like people.

Pessimists hate others.

Optimists like others.

Some everyday signs of hostility are touchiness, jealousy, rivalry, criticism.

Let's see how it works. Do you know someone who does not seem to like you? Have you ever done anything to make him dislike you? Maybe not. His dislike is simply his own hostility. He may be envious of your good job, jealous of your handsome profile.

Can he get you to do good work for him? Of course not! You will go through the motions, but you don't put your heart in it because you sense his hostility and may be returning it with interest.

But perhaps his dislike of you is not due to jealousy over your face or your job. You may have done something to show him up some time ago. That happens quite often and is almost always an expression of hostility. So

I Will...

1. Build men — big men.

2. Give everyone on the payroll an opportunity to advance if he is willing to pay the price in intelligent hard work.

3. Emphasize the human side of the organization and build morale in my company.

4. Recognize that modern business is a responsible public service, and that profit-making entails the developing of public good will and wider purchasing power with resulting general benefits.

5. Have a creative attitude of mind and use the research approach to every problem.

6. Follow the three R's of creative business thinking:

    Realism
    Research
    Resolute Reasoning

7. Have enthusiasm for change — courage for new ideas — daring of imagination and sincerity of conviction.

8. Cooperate with government regulations: Do everything possible to maintain the American Way of Life.

9. Have high standards and make no compromise with principle.

10. Have faith in God.

Harry A. Bullis

December 29, 1942

When Harry A. Bullis became president of General Mills, he "sunk his ships" by giving all employees this printed pledge. (See page 174.)

his dislike may be a reflection of the hostility that he senses is coming from you. He cannot have his heart in work for you so long as he senses a trace of hostility.

It is essential for the supervisor or salesman to like people. Those with traces of hostility have to work vastly harder for mediocre results.

At a meeting of aircraft supervisors I asked each man to write down the names of the three supervisors they judged to like people best. A month later I asked the same supervisors to write the names of the three they thought were most successful in handling people. The names were almost the same on both lists. When we like people we have better results leading them.

The pessimist can always find people to mourn with him about his troubles or about the dark outlook for the future. But you seldom hear of pessimists who get anything big done. They are better bellyachers than leaders. This is inevitable since pessimism is usually a form of ingrowing jealousy and distrust.

Teddy Roosevelt was no Pollyanna; he didn't close his eyes to what was wrong. He could see things that needed correction and did not hesitate to jump on them with both feet. But if he had a lurking envy or distrust as the basis for his constructive faultfinding, it was well concealed. He jumped on things optimistically, not destructively.

And he had a genuine helpfulness toward individuals, a liking for people, that prevented him from being anything but an optimist. His liking for people was shown by the way he encouraged them. Edward Bok relates how he received much encouragement from Teddy for projects he wanted to undertake but was not quite certain about. Bok would explain what he was contemplating to Roosevelt. Then did Roosevelt throw cold water on it, or appropriate the idea for himself? No.

"Go to it, you Dutchman!" was Teddy's encouraging exclamation.

Bok would depart from one of these sessions feeling optimistically as if he could move mountains.

Optimism thus begets optimism, in others as well as in oneself.

There is no better way to acquire optimism than to like people and give them some optimism.

To have OPTIMISM that GETS
ENTHUSIASM

Act optimistically
Smile—actually laugh
Like people, even pessimists

Act as if you were certain of success.

7

Tact that holds people

T he trouble in Washington," a high government official said, "is that so much of the work of our
bureaus requires high technical skill, and it is difficult
to find men who are both technically trained and tactful.
They do their work splendidly, until it comes to talking with the taxpayers."

I am afraid there is considerable truth in that statement. Engineers are not usually noted for their tact. The
president of one engineering college believes this situation is a handicap for his graduates. Yet he is tactful
enough not to tell them so bluntly. Instead, he arranges
a Town Hall Lecture Series for the students each year
and schemes to have several of the talks deal primarily
with getting along with people. Now don't jump to the
wrong conclusion that only those who have engineering
degrees could be more tactful.

Magnetic people especially need to watch their tact.
It is a paradox that their very attractiveness arouses envy
in others. The magnetic people must conduct themselves
so tactfully that this envy becomes loyal admiration.

Benjamin Thompson, for instance, was born a few
miles from Boston. His education was mostly what he
gave himself. Since he had a magnetic personality he
progressed rapidly. He even had a wealthy widow fall

in love with him and marry him before he was twenty. He always attracted people far above him in the world, in Boston, in England, and in Germany. He became Count Rumford, founder of the Royal Institution. Yet with all his progress and personality, life was stormy for him because his very personality and achievements aroused envy.

Personal magnetism will draw people to one; it takes tactfulness to hold them.

Want to cut your own throat? If you do, just forget how to be tactful.

There was Lloyd. He had had to fight for everything in life, and after he got himself through college and into a promising factory job, he kept right on fighting, instead of using tact.

He mastered his job quickly, was given more responsibility, and felt he was due for a raise. One day the boss called him to the office, and Lloyd felt in his bones it was about the raise. It was—in a way.

The boss told him he was doing a good job in every respect but one; he left too many ruffled feelings in his wake. He would get a raise, the boss said, when he found out how to work tactfully with people.

The boss himself was a self-made man. He told Lloyd how he, too, had been blunt rather than tactful. It had made him bereft of friends, almost lonesome. It had led others in the organization to try to knife him in the back. It had made him a poor boss back in those days, though he knew the business thoroughly.

Lloyd had always assumed that the big boss had been born tactful. It was a revelation—and an encouraging one —to find that the boss had had to learn how to be tactful.

Behind the closed doors of the private office, the friendly boss told Lloyd the four rules he had followed to develop his tact.

"The biggest raise we can ever give you," the boss said at the close, "is four rules to follow in your relations with others, whether in the shop, home, or on the street. Follow these four rules, and you will always leave people thinking better of themselves—and that is tact. Good luck!"

Here are the four positive rules that helped Lloyd and have helped many others.

1. *Treat everyone as if he were your superior*

Lloyd was proud of his self-earned engineering degree. You can't blame him. There were only a few other engineering graduates with the firm. Lloyd naturally felt a bit superior, but he did not conceal this feeling. He didn't go around openly bragging, but he did have a tendency to talk too much about college and to belittle those who were not college graduates. Instead, he should have kept his pride a secret.

The first rule that the boss gave him revolutionized his apparent attitude toward the people with whom he worked. He used to refer to the office messenger as "this good fellow." Now he calls him by his proper and full name. The messenger thinks Lloyd will make a good superintendent.

Lloyd formerly gave orders bluntly. Now he works in the tactful word "please" and puts a little extra emphasis on that word new to his vocabulary.

He used to say "thanks" occasionally, but it was mechanical and meaningless. No one seemed to hear it.

Now he says "thank you" for even little things. And he says it with the emphasis on the *you* part, like this: "Thank YOU!"

Formerly he interrupted others when they were talking, usually to impress them with the fact either that he knew it already or that he knew a whole lot more.

He used to call the girls by their first names or by nicknames he invented for them. This is always dangerous, and as he applied this rule he began to call them, properly, *Miss* Smith or *Miss* Brown.

And his sarcasm and ridicule vanished when he treated others as his superiors.

Tactlessness consists chiefly in doing little things that belittle or annoy others. We can't belittle, even unwittingly, when we treat all as though they were our superiors. Try it yourself and see.

Harry Selfridge was looked upon as a foreigner in London. True, he was a Michigan-born boy, trained with Marshall Field in Chicago, and trying to build one of the largest retail stores in all England. There was prejudice toward him, even among his own employees.

This former bundle boy overcame much of this prejudice by tactfully treating his salespersons as if they were his superiors. He did not call them "workers" or "shop assistants." He dignified them with the title of "members of the staff."

Young people often size up others from their clothes and treat them accordingly. Stylishly dressed people get the attention, those in plain clothes are given cold treatment. Perhaps this is because youth judges many things superficially, not looking for what is under the surface. Contrast these two historical incidents.

There was great excitement among the inhabitants of a Kentucky town. The surveyors for the Louisville & Nashville Railroad were laying tracks to their town. A sparse man, covered with spring mud, registered at the town's sole hotel. The clerk looked him over and assigned the frowsy-looking man to the poorest room.

In a few moments the man returned, asking for a better room.

"That room is plenty good for the looks of you," the clerk retorted.

The outraged "surveyor" seized the register and wrote across it in a large, bold hand: "Surveyors. Locate the road far enough away from Xville so they can barely hear the whistles." He signed his name, as president of the Louisville & Nashville.

Now come to a hotel in Philadelphia, at the time of a big convention, years ago. Hotels were jammed to overflowing. A plain-looking man and woman asked for a room at a small out-of-the-way hotel. They talked with a German accent and were obviously tired. The clerk felt sorry for these simple people.

"Our rooms are all taken," the clerk said, "but I will let you have my room and I will sleep on a cot tonight."

The man was John Jacob Astor. The clerk in the obscure hotel was George C. Boldt. Astor built the Waldorf-Astoria for Boldt and made him a millionaire.

"Whatever your customer's station of life," Sir Thomas Lipton instructed his employees, "whether he is proprietor, manager, head of a department, or only the owner of a one-horse show in a small village, make him feel that, for you, he is the one man in the universe."

John Wanamaker did this. As one of the best known and wealthiest men in the country, he would still stop and chat with the lowest employees and shabbiest customers. He could have been high-hat but was either too human or too wise to fall into that trap.

Abraham Lincoln was as deferential when talking to an office messenger as to his Secretary of State. He made himself one with all persons. One of his cabinet members said: "It is impossible to imagine anyone a valet to Mr. Lincoln; he would have been his companion."

In his early days Andrew Carnegie received unusual help from a blacksmith in some labor disturbance. The help was unexpected and unsolicited. "You were nice to me once in Pittsburgh," the blacksmith told him, "and now I can repay you."

"I have had many similar incidents in my life," Carnegie reported. "Slight attentions or a kind word to the humble often bring back rewards as great as they are unexpected. No kind action is ever lost."

Bertha is one of the most loyal and underpaid secretaries I know. Nothing would pry her loose from her job, however. When she enters her employer's office in the morning he not only says, "Good morning, Miss Bertha," but also stands and bows slightly.

There are two good old phrases that seem to have gone a bit out of fashion. They should be used more, by salespersons, employers, bosses, everyone. "If you please" is one phrase. Not just "please," but the whole thing, "if *you* please." Put the emphasis on the "you."

The other is "thank *you*," not "t'anks" or "much-abliged." And put the emphasis on the "you" part every time.

Don't take compliance for granted. Use these phrases as habitually as you say "hello" when starting a telephone conversation.

2. Consider the opinions, customs, whims, and prejudices of others

I used to enjoy telling stories about Negroes. I thought I was pretty good at duplicating a southern dialect and imagined my stories were a riot. To get acquainted with a new class years ago, I told a Negro story. It was a story I had always enjoyed, and it pointed a moral I wanted to get across to the class.

But this time I didn't enjoy the story. Neither did the class. The story was almost finished before I realized that there were two colored ministers in the back row. But then it was too late, and I limped on to the end of the story. A few students chuckled to please their teacher, but the silence was heavy as lead. The thing to do was to apologize for my poor taste, in front of the entire class.

The colored men were more tactful, and better sports, than their instructor. When I apologized, one of them said: "Oh, that's quite all right. You know, it reminded me of a story from Alabama." He told his story in a beautiful voice and won a thunder of applause from the class.

During the long cheering for him I made a silent resolve never again to tell a story on a Negro. I simply change the story to a Connecticut Yankee, and it is even

funnier and more plausible, unless I make it on a Scotsman with whiskers.

The same with stories and remarks about political and
religious groups, prohibitionists, and vegetarians. Many
people have firm convictions and are entitled to them.
We do not mind these unless we ourselves are opinionated in the opposite direction.

The tactful person is a tolerant person. It is painful
for the opinionated person to be tactful. He is always
stepping on someone's toes, often intentionally, and having his own stepped on in return. That is why most isms
make so few converts in proportion to the time and contributions put into the cause. They tactlessly fight ahead,
often making two enemies for each convert.

It is no accident that an aggressive Swede, Phil Johnson, chief of the Boeing Aircraft Co., has made his after-
dinner fame, not on Jewish or Scotch stories, but on
Swedish stories. They are all the funnier because a
Swede is telling them, and they do not affront his listeners.

And there is adaptable, considerate Thomas Lipton.
He traveled through Ireland and Scotland, buying pro-
visions for his growing chain of stores. Those countries
have dozens of dialects. Young Tom observed these,
practiced them. Then he would use the dialect of the
customer with whom he was talking. He made thousands of friends—and customers—by adapting himself to
their customs.

We must adapt ourselves to the other person's prejudices, too. When Josef Hofmann, the famous pianist,
became an American citizen he wanted to be a 100 per
cent American. So he decided to be true to his new

country by giving piano recitals of American composers' compositions, only. He spent a year practicing and preparing his all-American program. But American audiences did not like his selections; the foreign composers were so much better, you know.

What to do? In the next city the program was changed. The names of Mendelssohn, Schubert, and all the foreign favorites appeared. The auditorium was packed, the critics enthusiastic.

"Rubinstein has never been played so exquisitely," one critic said of a composition that was actually written by a Middletown, Conn., boy, Reginald De Koven.

Hofmann had merely tacked the names of foreign composers onto American works and thereby demonstrated the prejudiced opinion of American audiences.

A prominent businessman in the Middle West, who had inherited his prominence, found himself seated at a banquet beside a Chinese whose name he did not get. The local bigwig thought this was an insult to his family standing and showed a most condescending attitude toward the foreigner. He tried to carry on a conversation, using pidgin English, but did not get very far.

"Likee soupee?" he asked the foreigner. The Chinese nodded, and that was the end of their conversation.

When the speeches started, the bigwig was astonished to find that his foreign companion was the featured guest. It was Wellington Koo, who held the degree of doctor of philosophy from Columbia University and had been Chinese ambassador to France, England, Mexico, and the United States. He held his audience spellbound and used better English than the bigwig and all his ancestors could command. When Dr. Koo finished his talk and sat down, amid thundering applause, he turned to Mr. Bigwig, and asked, with that inscrutable smile of the Oriental, "Likee speechee?"

An American businessman, on his first trip abroad, was entertained by a gentleman in Damascus. Over their tiny cups of sirupy black coffee the gentleman of Damascus asked: "How does Damascus compare with your native Cleveland?"

"Oh, I suppose it's nice enough," the American said, "but in Cleveland we have more pep and zip. All over the United States, in fact, we move faster and get much more done than you do here."

"Ah, yes," sighed his host. "We tried that here two thousand years ago and gave it up."

The American go-getter had muffed another opportunity for being tactful.

Gladstone was a fighter but a tactful man. Someone asked, "How can he still be popular among those he fights?"

"Because he is always able to speak well on the subject in which his companion is most interested," the Duchess of Cleveland replied.

Specialists such as engineers may find it difficult to converse on topics outside their own special interest. People who are studying to become specialists could wisely cultivate the habit of reading in fields other than their own. This will keep their interests broad as well as help them to be tactful with people who are not specialists. Engineers are likely to be as tactful as a sledge hammer.

Alcibiades, the politician of ancient Athens, was by

nature luxury-loving and foppish in his habits. Yet he was wise enough in the ways of tact to hide his own interests and conform to the interests of others. Plutarch reports, for instance, that when Alcibiades visited the rigorous Spartans:

> By conforming to their diet and other austerities, he charmed and captivated the people. When they saw him bathing in cold water, feeding on their coarse bread, or eating their black broth, they could hardly believe that such a man had ever kept a cook in his house, visited the perfumer, or worn a robe of purple. It seems that, amongst his other qualifications, he had the extraordinary art of engaging the affections of those with whom he conversed, by imitating and adopting their customs and way of living. Thus, at Sparta, he was all for exercise, frugal in his diet, and severe in his manners.
>
> In Asia he was as much for mirth and pleasure, luxury and ease. In Thrace, again, riding and drinking were his favorite amusements, and in Persia he outvied the Persians themselves in pomp and splendor.
>
> Because he knew his native manners would be unacceptable to those whom he happened to be with, he immediately conformed to the ways and fashions of whatever place he came to.

That is applying the adage to do as the Romans do when in Rome.

A similar incident is told both of Queen Victoria and of Dolly Madison, the charming First Lady of President Madison's administration. The story could have been true of either of them. Anyway, a rustic person was paying the Queen or the President's wife a visit on official business. It being late afternoon, tea was served. The visitor was from that rugged section of the country where men do not like their drinks boiling hot, so he poured out a saucerful, blew noisily on it to lower the temperature, and then sipped it loudly.

And Dolly Madison—or it may have been Queen Victoria—is said to have shocked the attendants by saucering and blowing her tea after the custom of the guest.

This could have happened with Dolly Madison. Of her, Henry Clay said, "Everybody loves Mrs. Madison—and Mrs. Madison loves everybody."

It is often alleged that bankers are short on tact. Perhaps this is because they must of necessity say "No" to many would-be borrowers. But a banker in Texas, who became president of one of our air lines, was tactful. After a good crop year, a white-trash farmer found himself with several hundred dollars. He had never used a bank before but thought maybe he should put the cash in a safer place than the mattress.

Being strange to the ways of banking, he became uneasy a few days after he had deposited his stack of bills. He saddled his mule and rode to the bank, asking to look at his money for a bit. The banker, inwardly chuckling, ushered the new depositor into the directors' room and brought out the amount of his deposit for him to count. After the sharecropper had looked at it to his heart's content, he passed the money back, saying, "Reckon I'll let you keep it some more. Guess it's safe enough har, and that's a mighty purty room you let me look at it in."

That beat a half-hour discourse on the intricacies and perils of banking in keeping a customer happy.

The second rule of tact is that you should respect all customs of others, even in small matters. This not only makes you more tactful but also keeps you from becoming too opinionated.

Albert, heroic king of Belgium during the First World War, had real tact. A tribal chieftain from the Belgian Congo was being entertained in the royal palace.

"Tell me the music you like best," Albert asked as they listened to the royal orchestra after dinner.

A few minutes later the orchestra paused while a few of the musicians tuned their instruments.

"That's it," said the chief.

The remainder of the evening they listened to the orchestra tuning up.

King Albert had considered the opinions of others.

And in the Second World War our soldiers sent to foreign lands were carefully instructed to respect the customs and opinions of the people in these countries. Even those sent to England were given detailed information about the customs they would find there, so that they might avoid giving offence. After all, drinking cokes is as outlandish in British eyes as their tea drinking may seem to you.

But you do not have to go to foreign shores to find divergent opinions and customs. The people right in your own office or shop have them. And some are touchy about theirs. Never step on their toes intentionally; consider their opinions and you will not irritate them.

3. Use constructive "smile words" and phrases

If you wanted to ask a favor, would you depend upon your dignity and position, or a smile?

Senator Thomas C. Platt wanted the "Empire State Express" to stop for him at a small town near Buffalo. Usually that crack train only stops for a catastrophe. But the Senator used tact in the form of smile words. To the president of the railroad he wired:

> KINDLY HAVE EMPIRE STATE EXPRESS STOP HERE
> TO TAKE ON MRS. T. C. PLATT AND
>
> > ME TOO.

His smile-word ending of the request stopped the train!

The fish-market boy, reared in the slums, who became the first citizen of New York State, had the tactful art of using smile words to ease tactless situations. During hearings on a bill for the appointment, solely by the Governor, of an important board one speaker raised strong objection.

"We should have a safeguard provision that both political parties will be represented on this board," he urged.

"I don't think that is necessary," replied Governor Smith, a Democrat. The hearing chamber was tense; this seemed like the start of a fight. But the Governor went on, "There is no danger of my appointing a commission made up entirely of Republicans." There was nothing epoch-making about this joke, but it tactfully paved the way for a *non*partisan board. Al Smith won many of his victories over opposition by this tactful use of smile words.

Calvin Coolidge was not noted for his diplomatic tact, except for two attributes. For one thing, he didn't talk much, so he had few chances to say the tactless thing. For the other, he had a dry sense of humor, without the bitterness that is often characteristic of that kind of humor. There was the time, for instance, when he was still only president of the Massachusetts Senate, when, in the heat of argument, one senator advised another to go to hell.

"Mr. President," shouted the offended senator, "did you hear what my colleague said to me? I demand action!"

"I heard," Coolidge replied. "I've already looked up the law, and you don't have to go."

There is more to using smile words than having a sense of humor. For the humor treatment is dangerous if the joke is on another person.

Smile words are constructive words, pleasant words. Opposing them are the blunt, frank, unpleasantly harsh words. I feel that much of the opposition to bureaucrats arises, for instance, because they write letters and issue rulings in cold, blunt, legal words. Maybe red tape makes this necessary, but all too often a simple letter from a government bureau reads like a dangerous threat when it is nothing of the sort.

Engineers, too, like lawyers, have the unfortunate tendency to use blunt words rather than smile words. In one Pennsylvania plant a surly spirit was developing among the employees during the Second World War. It was difficult to know the cause of this, but I suspected

the blunt wording of announcements on bulletin boards
and in pay envelopes might be a factor. As the advertising manager had little work to do, I suggested that all
the notices and announcements be written in his department, using all the skill with constructive words that
would be used to prepare an advertisement for thousands
of prospective customers. He did not change the meanings of the announcements, but he did make them seem
less cold and harsh. The attitude of the employees
changed gradually, and nothing was done but have a
word expert rather than an engineering expert prepare
the notices.

During butter rationing I was in a store where the
customers were huffing and puffing against the restric-
tions. The clerk at the dairy counter told each customer
he could have *only* half a pound of butter.

A few days later I was in Jim Walsh's store. When I
asked for butter, he smiled and said, "We can let you
have *as much as* half a pound." That sounded like a lot
more than only half a pound.

The manager of the dress-goods department of a dry-
goods store wanted to cut down on the overhead costs
per sale. He set up a limitation on the size of the piece
goods to be sold. The first few weeks this backfired and
cut into sales volume. Investigation showed this unexpected result was due to the way the salesgirls gave this
information to the customers.

"You can buy no less than a yard," they were telling
customers. That was negative.

They were instructed to say, "You can buy as little
as one yard." That produced a change in the customers'
attitude toward the limitation.

Almost anything can be stated pleasantly, or unpleasantly. We can tell a person he is a liar—or tactfully say he has overlooked some facts.

We can call him the janitor—or the custodian.

We can speak of death—or of slipping away; of being stingy—or of being thrifty; of being a gossip—or of having insatiable curiosity; of being fired—or of terminating services.

We can say the product is a *substitute* for the one the customer wants—or call it the *successor*.

We can call an employee our Man Friday—or our assistant.

We can say the job is dirty—or that it is no job for a dude.

Pessimists tend to use grouch words. Optimists use smile words just as naturally. Many business deals fall through, many employees are disgruntled, because grouch words were used rather than constructive smile words.

Glenn Martin had just turned twenty and was starting in business for himself at Santa Ana, Calif. He had moved there from the Middle West, because of his mother's poor health. The savings from his work as an automobile repairman were put into renting an unused church. In this church he went to work building an airplane. This was just a couple of years after the first successful flight of the Wright brothers at Kitty Hawk. Young Martin had built many large kites back in Kansas, but this was his first attempt at an airplane. There were endless headaches in its construction.

TactLESS Expressions

Some common phrases that had better be changed or avoided.

"I don't want to criticize, but . . ."

"While it's none of my business, still . . ."

"Well, I warned you that . . ."

"It's time to be frank, so . . ."

"We're good friends, so I can . . ."

"I may be wrong, but . . ."

"Don't ever repeat this, but . . ."

"Excuse me if this hurts your feelings, but . . ."

"I shouldn't interfere, but if I . . ."

"I don't ordinarily gossip, but . . ."

"Someone should tell you, and . . ."

"Far be it from me to discourage you, but . . ."

"I think you're man enough to take this . . ."

The real headache came, however, when he was ready to take the machine out of the church and see if it would actually fly. The machine was too big to get through the church doors.

Should he knock out a hole in the church and run the risk of a lawsuit? Young Martin used smile words and solved this headache.

"When I clean up my work," he said to the landlord, "how would you like to have me enlarge the church entrance and put in a spacious vestibule?"

"Fine—that is, if you don't charge me for it!"

Charge him for it? Why, that new entrance would be vastly cheaper, and quicker, than tearing his machine apart to get it outside.

Martin got what he wanted by using smile words in terms of the landlord's own self-interests. He offered to do the landlord a favor, instead of asking a special privilege.

What unpleasant things have you had to talk about today? Think back, and figure out how you could have talked about them in a more constructive, tactful way.

Make it an unvarying policy to handle unpleasant things by using smile words.

4. *Feel friendly*

Some people are tactless because they are careless or thoughtless. Others are tactless because of their own concealed envy or hostility. It is the same hostility with which we became acquainted in the previous chapter.

I shall never forget my first purchase in a store in the Deep South. The charming young woman wrapped my purchase, handed me my change, and said, "*Do* come back and see me sometime!"

Were my ears deceiving me? She didn't try to sell me something else. She just looked at me with her beautiful blue eyes and asked me to come and see her again. Well, I wondered, maybe the girls down here like whiskers. Maybe I'm more attractive than I had figured. Secretly, I wished I had put on my best suit, if that was the way she felt.

Down the street I stopped at another store. A middle-aged gentleman waited on me. I mean "gentleman." He wrapped my purchase, gave me my change, and said:

"Thank you, Sir, and *do* come back and see me again!"

So that was it! I hadn't made a personal hit, after all, with the charming blue-eyed woman. She talked that way to all her customers.

That friendly "*Do* come back and see me again" is the universal phrase in stores in the Deep South. It gives the parting customer a friendly pat on the back. It is a tactful way to end one transaction so that the door is left invitingly open for the next.

George, my friend, makes a machine that is used in automobile service stations. It costs quite a bit of money but is worth it, so he tells me. A few weeks ago he knew I was to be in Ohio on a lecture tour. "If you get to X town, you can collect a bill for me," he said. "I sold one of our machines to a service station there, and the owner still owes for most of it. Guess the old man is having a tough time, so we haven't pressed him. You know how rationing has cut into the service station business. I wonder about his two boys, who used to work with him. They're probably in service now."

"Will you give me 20 per cent if I collect the bill while I am there?" I asked, half jokingly.

"I'll give you half if you can collect it," he replied.

I looked in the classified section of the telephone book in X town a few days later. The filling station in question was just a few blocks from the hotel, and I enjoyed the walk to it in the brisk fall air.

As the filling station came in sight I noticed a service flag, with two stars, hanging in the window.

"Hello," I said to the proprietor, who was counting gasoline coupons. "I'm a friend of George's, over in Connecticut."

"Uh-huh," he replied, continuing to count stamps.

"George was wondering about you last Sunday. Wanted to know about your boys," and I pointed toward the service flag.

"Wait till I get my other specs on," he replied, as he turned toward me and started to rise. So he told me about his boys, both airplane mechanics then. He showed me their pictures in uniform. He got so excited that his nose started to drip. After he told me that he hadn't heard from one of the boys for six weeks he wiped the drip from his nose and surreptitiously from the corner of his eyes.

"I've wondered, too, about George," he went on. "Figured his business was just about gone, unless he was in war production. Well, it's not so easy for any of us. We got a war to win as fast as we can. But ain't it just like George, to be awondering about my boys when he's probably got enough troubles of his own."

When I got back from the trip George called me up.

"What did you do?" he exclaimed. "Did you hypnotize that fellow? I've a letter from him, in pencil. Says he had a nice visit with a feller with whiskers, and he enclosed a check for part of his account. He wrote that he'd send some each month, from the government money the boys send, until the bill is settled. What magic did you use on him?"

No magic at all. Just the tact of friendliness. I had not mentioned the debt.

And, oh, yes!, George turned out to be a piker. When I pressed him, he said 50 per cent was pretty stiff for collecting a bad account so easily. So we compromised. That explains why the Community Chest in X town received an unexpected check for half of the bad account.

You remember how Franklin D. Roosevelt was elected over Herbert Hoover? You might expect the vanquished to have no more than a lukewarm friendliness for the victor.

Mrs. Hoover attended a dinner party during F.D.R.'s third term, and the conversation turned to a series of criticisms of Mrs. Roosevelt.

Mrs. Hoover leaned to her companion and whispered, "Get into the conversation with a loud voice and change the subject."

She was the loser, yet she felt tactfully friendly.

A young woman writer, gaining fame rapidly for her sophisticated writing, was invited to a fashionable tea. Walking up the steps to the brownstone mansion, she noticed the society lady ahead of her had the seams in her stockings twisted.

"Oh, I must tell her about that," the writer said to her sponsor.

"No, don't. She may take a dislike to you for calling a fault to her attention," the sponsor advised. "Anyway, that looks like a last year's dress she is wearing."

But the excited writer, eager to get on in society, quickened her steps and said to the woman with the twisted hosiery, "I beg your pardon, but did you know that is last year's dress you are wearing!"

What a humiliating slip of the tongue! The young woman seemed to have good intentions, but the slip of her tongue betrayed her hostility to society women.

Friendliness is more than using the right words. The friendly feeling has an essential inner spirit. Many inadvertent, tactless remarks that slip out, and are deeply regretted, reflect hostility rather than friendliness.

Magnetic Alexander Hamilton drew people to him, but he couldn't keep them with him. He had personal magnetism but lacked tact because of his lurking hostility.

On the other hand, Benjamin Franklin wore well, his attractiveness lasted, because he was genuinely friendly and could not help being tactful.

And Lloyd, whom we were discussing at the beginning of this chapter, had been hard-pressed financially all his life. He envied anyone who had been born in comfortable circumstances. He was blunt and inconsiderate when talking to, or about, people who had not had to struggle for a start in this world.

It had not occurred to Lloyd that he was not genuinely friendly. But it is to his lasting credit that he tried to become friendly to all, and succeeded. He found it more fun than going around with his back up. He discovered that others returned this friendliness, just as they had been reflecting his slight hostility.

He began to laugh with people, not at them.

He made himself seem enthusiastic when he ran across acquaintances on the street.

He began to look for the good points in people and to mention these in a complimenting fashion. He formerly told the elevator girl that the company had designed a good uniform for her, but he now told her that she made the uniform look good. People he used to call "old fossils" he now calls "mature" or "experienced," combining friendliness with smile words.

He now goes out of his way to do thoughtful little things for others, not just for important people, as he used to do stiffly.

There is an interesting aspect of this lurking hostility that destroys tact. Men are more apt to be tactless when dealing with men than with women. In the case of women, this is reversed.

Friendliness made Teddy Roosevelt seem tactful even when he was smashing away with the big stick. Lack of tact made Woodrow Wilson seem coldly blunt when using words that might have been tactful, but Wilson did not seem to feel friendly. This lack kept Wilson from being the leader he might have been, though he had the highest position in our country.

There are many in positions of responsibility throughout the country who are not the leaders they could otherwise be, for the same reason. There are many skilled in their work who do not get an opportunity to take over responsibility, simply because they need to learn to be tactful.

Ninety-five out of a hundred can learn tactfulness with only slight effort. The other five may find it a hopeless job. These are the chaps who have chips on their shoulders. They have to get rid of those chips first.

Every boss is a broadcaster, whether he realizes it or not. When he speaks to one worker, others hear and are affected by what is said although the remarks were not intended for them.

The employee's wife and family are likely to hear about it.

Soon neighbors know what the boss said.

Whether the boss likes it or not, he should fully comprehend the significance of this. Even his casual comments, intended for only one person, might as well be broadcast over a loud-speaker system. Such a system, in fact, might be preferable, for at least that would not distort the boss's comments and give them changed meanings.

The real leaders realize this and guard all their remarks tactfully. Some have to learn this the hard way.

Some of Thomas A. Edison's earliest inventions dealt with the telegraph, and his first big sales were to Western Union. But then something happened, and Western Union would no longer buy a thing Edison produced. Why? Here is the reason in Edison's own words.

One day I was sitting in Jay Gould's office chatting with him. He began to complain that Western Union was not expanding its business as rapidly as he thought it should. He couldn't understand why it didn't go ahead faster.

"Well, Mr. Gould," I said, "I can tell you the

reason. The trouble is that you have a man at the head of it who doesn't understand the business. You can't make progress without improvement, and General Eckert opposes and blocks every proposal of that kind. What you need is a new general manager."

Gould and I were sitting with our backs to one of the entrance doors to his office and neither of us noticed that Eckert's secretary had entered the room until we turned around and saw him standing before the desk. He had heard every word I said, as I learned afterwards, and reported it to Eckert. From that time forward my goose was cooked with Eckert. He won't use anything with my name attached to it."

But whether it is such eavesdropping, or the natural interest in repeating what the boss said, the would-be leader must always bear in mind that he is as good as shouting through a megaphone whenever he opens his mouth.

Tactfulness has far-reaching consequences for the boss.

For TACT in SMOOTHING THE WAY

Treat everyone as if he were your superior
Consider their opinions, whims, prejudices
Use constructive smile words and phrases
Swap envy for friendliness

8

Keeping progressive and out of the rut

Some 300,000 businesses are discontinued each year. Why? Is it unfair competition, lack of opportunity, or dishonesty?

Most of these small businessmen—manufacturers, storekeepers—have to go out of business because they are set in their ways. The official records report it as "poor management," which is a tactful way of saying that most of them were in ruts and would not change their business methods to meet the changed conditions.

And conditions are ever changing—new machinery, new methods, new materials, new laws, new competitors, new employees, new customers. Change is inevitable.

The leaders not only cooperate with these changes and take fullest advantage of them; they also help bring about still more changes, while the die-hards, on the other hand, struggle to keep their businesses just the same, at the same old locations, and complain about the modern notions that ruin business.

A moss-backed storekeeper in a backwoods locality fired his young clerk. Now the clerk was an eager young chap, ambitious and full of new ideas he wanted to try out in the store. But the owner fired young Harry. Soon Harry Gordon Selfridge had a good new job.

And, like a story from Horatio Alger, Gordon Self-ridge won fame and fortune with Marshall Field in Chicago. Then he opened his own great store in London, which revolutionized the store methods of that nation of storekeepers. Someone told the old storekeeper who had fired young Selfridge about his meteoric rise.

"Wal-l-ll. It's purty hard to believe," the old store man commented. "You know, he didn't amount to much when he worked for me."

Sometimes corporations get into a rut. This starts as dry rot in the higher executives. It occurs most frequently in firms that depend upon exclusive patents or upon some apparent monopoly of natural resources.

Years ago, for example, Western Union Telegraph Company had a chance to buy the telephone for $100,-000. But the directors of the telegraph company felt too secure in their own patents back there in 1876 and were not progressive enough to see the future possibilities of the telephone. They ignored the upstart invention. The telephone became worth billions, not millions, and eventually controlled Western Union.

People get into such ruts because they turn their minds to the past. *They regress.*
The leader looks ahead. HE PROGRESSES.

You'd be astonished to learn how far some people can regress. I have worked with many who let the lure of the past overcome them. There was a woman who had been a schoolteacher, a well-built, attractive woman in her early fifties. But she did her hair in pigtails, wore school dresses. She lisped and used baby talk. The sanitarium officials humored her, and allowed her to wear big wide hair ribbons and to play with dolls.

There are a lot of people who have turned time back that way, who have regressed to their childhood make-believe living. But you seldom chance across them in daily life, since they are usually locked up for safekeeping.

Time cannot be turned back. It cannot be stopped or even slowed down.

Yet many folk who are not locked up try to turn it back in one way or another.

There is a young commercial artist of considerable promise, for instance. He claims that modern painters are no good and that manufacturers no longer make really good woolen cloth.

And there is an attorney who insists upon using an old-fashioned roll-top desk, has his office clerk add with a pad and pencil rather than an adding machine, wishes the telephone had never been invented. He is beginning to think, however, that the typewriter is probably here to stay.

There are many foremen and executives who boil inwardly when they have to adopt a new method. Many small plants are filled with antiquated, hand-feed machines that they are too moss-backed to replace with automatic-feed machines. These regressive attitudes spoil the foremen's and executives' chances for leadership and cause the plants to lose business to competitors.

Since people who are in ruts are invariably failures, some folk have erroneously concluded that unlucky breaks give people this attitude. But disappointments need not make one turn backward. They should prod one to move forward, to overcome the obstacle or failure.

Rowland Macy, from Nantucket, for instance, tried to be a storekeeper when he was nineteen—and failed. Then he followed the gold rush to California and set up a store at Marysville—and failed. Back in New England, he set up shop at Haverhill—failed.

So he jumped from the frying pan right into the fire and set up a two-by-four store between a drugstore and a stove store, in the noisiest, dirtiest part of New York City, on Sixth Avenue. Failed? No. In a couple of years he expanded. He had not let his mistakes and failures make him bitter. He learned from them. R. H. Macy & Co. is today one of the world's largest department stores, so progressive that it is profoundly hated by all its competitors.

The most forward-looking person I know is a man who has had a long, long life, filled with one disappointment after another. He could be a regressive failure if anyone could, but Uncle Will will not let himself tamper with time.

He has spent his nearly ninety years in the old farmhouse in which his ancestors lived for two centuries before him. But, like its present owner, it is the most modern house in the locality. The wear of years is on its exterior, but it was the first to have a telephone, a furnace, modern plumbing, electricity, bottled gas. "Young" Will was the first in his community to have a farm tractor, although he kept his oxen for a few years "to haul the tractor out when it bogged down." He recently staged a whirlwind one-man campaign to get the township fire department modernized.

Yet he has been seared by disappointment. His marriage was childless. His wife died years ago, in the bloom of young womanhood. Before that, it was his younger brothers who had the chance to go to college, and they all won fame in their professions, while Will stayed home to work so that they could go to college. The family money was wasted away by a dissolute relative.

For ten years now Uncle Will has been the last of his line. Is he a lonely old man, bitter and carping? Not Uncle Will.

He has "adopted" whole families of young people in his neighborhood. He remembers their birthdays and hops into his station wagon to wish them happy returns in person. He has helped out in their love affairs. He has helped many through college, just as he helped his brothers many years before.

I sat on the stoop of his hilltop home at sundown recently, watching spellbound as the fading rays of the sun were replaced by the twinkling man-made stars on the streets of the big city five miles away.

"It didn't use to be beautiful like that," he told me. "The sun would go down and the city would be lost. But electricity has brought it to life at dusk. It will be even more beautiful when there are more neon lights."

Looking ahead, not behind! Uncle Will is not in a rut, though most of his neighbors may be.

Uncle Will will not let the moss catch up with him. Neither would another Yankee, Dr. G. Stanley Hall, who was the grand old man of American psychology. Dr. Hall looked ahead. In his eighties, Dr. Hall learned to eat with chopsticks, took dance lessons to keep up with the new steps. He might be near the grave, but he would not let himself get into one of those graves that is open at both ends, a rut.

Retiring never occurred to Peter Cooper. His restless mind was still actively engaged in new inventions, new applications of science, when he was ninety years old. He kept looking ahead.

Michelangelo looked ahead and did some of his best work in his eighties.

Some neglect to look ahead as young men, when the future should be spread out on their horizon. There were the two brothers, Heinrich and John, both German immigrants in the early days of this republic. Heinrich landed first and started a butcher shop in New York. He did well enough and was entirely satisfied with himself, thank you. But John, the younger brother, restlessly looked to the future.

In those days Milwaukee was a flourishing pioneer city. Chicago was merely a small settlement of cabins around Fort Dearborn. Westward, there was nothing except scout trails and a few scattered outposts. Yes, maybe Heinrich was right to play safe where he was, in Little Old New York, then a city of 30,000 inhabitants.

But John saw more than blockhouses. He looked ahead and visualized the growth of the country. He got into a business that took him, on foot, over trails to the outposts of our civilization. He got acquainted with the savages and with the country and its few frontiersmen citizens. His fortune would be staked there.

To redheaded Thomas Jefferson, President of the United States, John pointed out on maps locations for great cities of the future. Chicago, the twin cities of Minnesota, Duluth, were merely blank spaces on that map.

But John Jacob Astor was looking forward, visualizing the future. He staked his future on the future.

Heinrich remained a comfortable butcher, reluctantly loaning money to his visionary brother to engage in new ventures in places that were not marked on any maps—and the money was always repaid.

John Jacob Astor could have used the motto Cyrus H. K. Curtis followed: "Yesterday ended last night."

We are going to meet Captain Robert Dollar again, but let's look at him now. He is eighty, erect, lithe, with his hair and eyebrows snowy white. His famous long goatee bobs merrily as he talks to companions at quaint India House, in New York City. He is surrounded by world traders, agog over the news that this patriarch is now starting a world-wide line of steamships for both freight and passenger service, the first of its sort and scope in the world.

An importer recognizes him and comes over to greet the energetic octogenarian.

"Always going at a good clip, eh! Captain," was his greeting. "Why don't you take it easy?"

Dollar's eyes twinkled. "Oh, you young fellows can afford to go slowly. You've probably got at least forty more years to live and do your work, but I'll be lucky to live twenty more. So, you see, I have to jump twice as fast as you young fellows!"

Robert Dollar was partly wrong. He did not have twenty more years; he died eight years later. But you can safely bet he died looking ahead.

Another progressive eighty-year-old, Henry G. Davis, the Grand Old Man of West Virginia, was riding through the empire he had built, accompanied by a younger man, who had retired.

"We used up the spruce off this tract for pulpwood," Mr. Davis told him as they came to a vast expanse of mountainside. "Now I'm replanting it with hickory. That's a mighty useful tree."

"How long does it take a hickory to grow before it can be used?"

"Oh, around forty years. Hickory can always be used and it should be kept growing."

He was looking ahead, not for himself, but for others.

The younger man, who thought he had retired, went back into business.

Oliver Wendell Holmes, Jr., was born into Boston's aristocracy. He did not need to work but spent a long life at it. In the War between the States he was badly wounded several times and went back for more each time. That was his life, always going back for more. For twenty-four years he served on our Supreme Court.

When he was eighty, reporters asked him how about retiring.

"I always thought that when I got to be eighty," he told them, "I could wrap up my life in a scroll, tie a pink ribbon around it, put it away in the drawer, and go around•doing the things I wanted to do. But I learned that when you have taken one trench there is always a new firing line beyond."

After the close of court, one day when he was ninety-one, he said to the attendant who was helping him with his overcoat, "I won't be in tomorrow." That was all the fanfare he wished when announcing his retirement at last.

Thomas Masaryk went to work as a blacksmith's helper. In the First World War he helped establish the Republic of Czechoslovakia and became its first president. And a quarter of a century later, at the age of eighty-four, he was again serving as president of the country he helped establish. A writer suggested it was time for Dr. Masaryk to take life easy.

"We think more of how we can lengthen life than how we can fill it," said the man who started his career at the anvil. "Many people take no account of the fact that they themselves are really living only half a life. We must do more than increase life—we must increase its worth.

"There is a dream that often comes back to me. I see a ship on the sea and an angel bending over it with an hourglass; and every now and then a drop runs down from the hourglass into the sea, and the angel says, 'Another minute passed away.' I always think of that dream as a warning: work, do something, while your minutes are passing."

It is not disappointments, nor age, that make one an old fogey. Eighteen is as dangerous an age for regression as eighty. Dr. Annette C. Washburne, at the University of Wisconsin, has studied those personality traits which show that a person has regressive tendencies, is headed for a rut.

The five most dangerous rut-digging personality traits are:

Keeping to oneself.
Having sensitive feelings.
Being intolerant of others' opinions.

Being bound by tradition.

Worrying.

People who show those traits are set against changes; they try to keep time from moving on. But time goes on and they are left behind.

Uncle Will does not keep to himself. He has lived alone in a big house for the past quarter century, but he visits a dozen families each day and has a station wagon to lug guests in and out.

He is tolerant of the opinions of others. Some of his closest friends are of foreign birth and have different religions and traditions. He makes changes to keep up with them.

He is not tradition-bound. He has changed his methods of farming dozens of times. He attends short courses at the state agricultural college. He keeps up with popular science books and books on world affairs. A few years ago he shut up shop completely to take a world cruise.

He has had plenty cause for worry but shrugs it off with a smile or a droll Yankee witticism and keeps right on forging ahead.

Perhaps the strongest force that keeps people in ruts is being tradition-bound. This is shown by such every-day statements as:

"We have always done it this way."

"The younger generation is going to the dogs."

"Oh, that's just a fad."

"Schools teach too many frills nowadays."

"We've always made money by doing it this way."

"Long hours of work were better—kept folks out of mischief."

"Let's not be too hasty."

"Woman's place is in the home."

"Let the other fellow try it first."

"Banks are getting too big."

"Now, when I was a young fellow . . ."

"We don't have craftsmen like they used to make."

"We had a big year three years ago."

"It's getting harder to do business every year."

"My father taught me how to run the business."

"There used to be more opportunities."

"Why read about my business?"

The ties that bind one to the past may hog-tie personal progress. Many people find it difficult to wean themselves from the past, yet it is essential if one is to keep out of the rut.

I often pass within a few miles of my boyhood town in Indiana but suppress the desire to stop off and relive the past.

After twenty years of college teaching, I broke away abruptly and completely. While teaching, I never taught the same course twice in the same way. It would have been easier to repeat the same things year after year, but I chose the hard way, to keep out of an academic rut. It was work, but it paid off.

When I moved from a town, I disposed of any property there as quickly as possible, even at a loss. Any loss in immediate cash received was more than offset by not being tradition-bound to the past.

The books and articles that I wrote ten years ago I ignore. Instead, I am planning the ones to write after this one.

When I found I was considered a specialist in one field, I intentionally broke off for another and am irritated when people remind me of the work of an earlier year. This has kept me from getting a swelled head and forced me to look to the future rather than gaze on the past.

Some people may have the good fortune of being just naturally progressive. Maybe Uncle Will is such a person; he doesn't watch the parade go by but is in the parade himself. I am one of those folks who have to work at being progressive. And I have a lot of company.

At a recent industrial conference, for instance, there were production men from more than a hundred firms. Most of them could fairly be called "progressive" industrial executives (the rut-bound don't go out looking for new ideas for their businesses).

"How many of you," I asked them, "honestly have to *force yourselves* to keep up with new developments in your industry?"

The majority of men in the crowded room raised hands. They had acquired their progressiveness by effort and were keeping it by effort.

They were showing self-leadership, intentionally leading themselves to keep out of ruts.

Do you know people who will not permit any rearrangement of their furniture? That is a sign that they are in a rut. You may know others who never vary from their daily routines—another dangerous sign. And some of these faithful, dependable workers never become more than that. Their regularity is a rut symptom. They don't change in little things and are likely to resist important changes.

I know of one family that deliberately makes little changes, just to keep away from the edge of a rut. In most families, for instance, the head of the house always carves the roast and fills the plates. But in this household sometimes the mother serves, at other times the children. They also change their regular places at the table from time to time.

Those children—and parents—are not likely to get into the condition of the ninety-year-old Texas frontiersman with eyes like poached eggs.

"You must have witnessed a great many changes," a visitor said to him.

"Yep," the old sourdough replied, "an' I resisted all of them just as long as I could!"

Strange as it may seem, there is more real danger of a specialist getting into a rut than there is for an ordinary person. Specialists keep their noses so close to the grindstone in their own narrow fields that they fail to notice the things that are happening in the world. They keep learning more and more, about less and less, until they finally know everything about nothing. The rest of the parade goes by and they don't even hear the band.

The specialist is wise to keep up in his reading on other fields.

I sometimes bring this point home to audiences by demonstrating a museum piece, a pair of red-flannel underdrawers. These prickly woolens symbolize the rise and fall of an industrial city of some 100,000 population. The city became a city of specialists. They dominated the world in making red flannels. The city's big plants were textile mills dedicated to red flannels. The bigwigs of the place looked down their noses at the small plants that were not making woolens.

Then heavy underwear began to go out of style.

"People will be getting pneumonia, wholesale," some flannel makers said.

"This flimsy rayon underwear, it's positively immoral," others chimed in.

But the flimsy underwear kept coming in while the heavy stuff declined.

"Maybe we need some more tariff protection," they began to shout. "Maybe advertising might help us," others suggested.

But the tide had turned, and my specimen set of red underwear is one of the last they made in that city. Some of the mills are in decay. Others were sold for a song and used for other manufacture. A few mill owners had enough cash reserve to be able to get machinery for making that immoral flimsy underwear.

The city had hard going, for years, because the managers of the woolen mills did not see what was going on right under their noses. They looked down their aristocratic noses at the very plants that showed them their real competition.

There was that small plant, for instance, which made automobile mufflers. Their young engineers developed an automobile heater that doubled their business. Did that affect the underwear business? Those in a rut couldn't see how, but it was a sign that people were riding in warm cars in cold weather, not in open sleds exposed to the untempered weather.

That sporty, ambitious upstart who had a still smaller plant in which he made custom-built bodies for rich men's automobiles was upsetting their red-flannel business, too. He devised ingenious features that helped make enclosed automobile bodies possible.

And that small foundry—foundrymen are so dirty, you know, my deah!—was changing from stovemaking and bringing out a new type of inexpensive furnace. They put advertising behind it and doubled their plant facilities. That was competing with red flannels; people were living in warmer homes.

The times were changing. There was evidence right in their own back yards, in the small plants that they had ignored.

Had the red-flannel people been alert, looking for changes, progressive, broad, they would have observed these changes and saved their firms—yes, saved their city a fifteen-year period of unusual hardships. But they wore blinders and watched only their own little business.

That is the danger ahead of every specialist. He has to keep his eyes on other fields.

He must watch for changes and adapt himself to them quickly, uncomplainingly.

As a business old-timer told a group of us, with the deepest sincerity: "The war has been a splendid thing for my plant, after all. I cussed at the outset over all the changes we had to make. But let me tell you, mister, I didn't know how deep a rut we were in. The war jerked us out of it."

Above all, look straight ahead to the future, glancing only occasionally over your shoulder at the past.

At his deathbed, friends were recalling to Cecil Rhodes, who made an empire in Africa, the many things he had accomplished. The wan man started to speak. His friends listened intently, for these might be his last words.

"So little done, so much left to do," Cecil Rhodes said as he went forward into the next world.

The forward look of the leader, even to death.

Some corporations that have been habit-bound and tradition-ridden have been jerked into forward-looking attitudes by smart new leaders who were called in to save them from insolvency. One of the most effective methods in these instances is to have all executives and foremen file reports, reports that do not review the work of their departments the past year, but that give the plans they are making for the coming year.

This forces the forward look upon them, for a while at least.

Unfortunately, too many have to have it forced on them.

Here is a little rule-of-thumb test for you to try:

How old are you?

People with a tendency to regress say, "I'm twenty-nine now."

Progressive people, with the forward look, say, "I'll be thirty next birthday."

Look forward, in all things.

```
Keeping PROGRESSIVE for LEADING
                OTHERS
     Mingle with others
     Keep your feelings insensitive
     Be tolerant of others' opinions
     Look ahead; think ahead
     Use effort to keep ahead of the times
```

*The successful executive looks two ways—to the past
to study experience, to the future to apply it.*

*On the right is another page of helpful maxims, which can be
removed and placed where you can look at them daily.*

A Personality *for* Leadership

Rules for Power over Others

by DR. DONALD A. LAIRD

BE BRISK.

THINK ABOUT THE OTHER PERSON.

ACT OPTIMISTICALLY.

TREAT ALL AS IF THEY WERE YOUR SUPERIORS.

USE CONSTRUCTIVE WORDS.

STIMULATE CREATIVE THINKING.

MAKE YOURSELF LIKE EVERYONE.

BE ACTIVE.

BE TOLERANT.

BE CONSIDERATE.

9

Starting initiative early

I was talking with the dean of the businessmen in a large eastern city about the self-made men in his locality. We had written down a rather long list of such men when he suddenly stopped.

"Say," he exclaimed with a circulating smile, "this is an easier job than picking out the men who started with money and managed to hold on to it. Not until I started to talk with you did I realize what a small percentage who were 'born successful' have remained successful. Look at the length of this list! Why, self-made men are almost a dime a dozen."

Then his expression clouded.

"Isn't it a downright shame," he continued, "that inheritance taxes and all that falderal make it impossible for a man to hold on to what is rightfully his? It isn't right."

But the answer may not be that simple. There is much more than taxes and regulations to consider.

Old residents like to boast about the past glories of Lafayette's mansion. They can tell romantic tales of Sunday afternoons when people from miles around drove past the mansion to admire the ornamental iron fence brought up from New Orleans, the gingerbread work on the wide cornices, the thoroughbred horses and shiny carriages in the stables. They still envy the Shet-

135

land pony and Dalmatian dogs with which Lafayette's children played.

A half century or so ago, everyone in the town envied those fortunate children who could have such a home. Surely those youngsters would be successful.

But today the old house tells a different story. The fence is rusted and crumpled. The croquet court is buried with underbrush. Sagging timbers from the big barn have been used by the neighborhood boys for Independence Day bonfires. The walnut paneling of the house is covered with spider webs and mold. Bats and owls fly around the winding staircase, down which once glided gorgeous girls to their expectant escorts.

"How could Lafayette's children ever allow such a beautiful place to go to ruins?" one asks the townspeople.

"None of 'em ever amounted to much," is the answer. "Don't know what old Lafayette would say about his offspring if he were alive today—a better man than he never walked this earth.

"One of the sons tried to run the factory after his father died, but couldn't keep it running.

"The unmarried daughter was a bit queer. Lived all alone in the big old house for years. They took her to the poor farm after the stairway collapsed. The youngest boy, the handsome one, hasn't been heard from for years; they say he took to drink.

"The third boy is working in an insurance office. He bought a bungalow on the other side of town and is paying for it on a government loan.

"The daughter who 'disgraced the family' by marrying a high-school teacher is living in Kansas. Her husband is school superintendent there. They say she has a son who is the spittin' image of his grandfather, who built the old showplace. Only hope he may have some of his grandpop's 'git up and git,' as well as his looks.

"Old Lafayette made this town. He started with a little shop, kept trying new ideas—was full of the derndest ideas you ever heard of—and first thing we knew he had built an up-and-coming factory. Half of the folks in town worked for him. He made a mint of money, built that elegant mansion, and had all the womenfolk in town trying to copy the new contraptions he kept finding for his no-good youngsters."

Many old mansions tell a similar story.

Lafayette's initiative made him, his town, and the townspeople. But it broke his children. He raised them with the same autocratic initiative that built his business, and he thus deprived his children of initiative of their own. He was too good a provider for his family. He kept them so comfortably satisfied that they lost any initiative he had not autocratically squeezed out of them.

The decayed mansion is a monument to the decay that can come to a family when initiative wanes. Autocratic old Lafayette loved his children but handled them so they did not have the combined initiative to carry on in his shoes. His attorney had sensed this and had urged Lafayette to leave his property in trust for them. By this time Lafayette was in his dotage, however, and was suspicious of newfangled financial ideas.

John D. Rockefeller, Sr., in encouraging contrast, kept initiative alive among his children. If he was autocratic, it was in the right direction; he made his children look out for themselves. There has been no decay of initiative in his son or grandsons.

An orphan boy was taking a test in a psychological clinic. The pencil slipped from his fingers, rolled across the table, and fell on to the floor with a plop. The orphan watched passively as the pencil rolled to a wavering stop. He made no effort to stop it or to pick it up after it had stopped itself.

This set the psychologist to wondering. Why didn't this lad have enough initiative to stop the pencil? Had the orphanage trained the initiative out of the boy?

The psychologist got fifteen other normal children from orphanages to see what they would do when their pencils started to roll away. Nine out of the fifteen sat like bumps on a log and let them roll.

Then he tried it with children who lived with their own families. Every last one of these children tried to stop the rolling pencils.

The orphanages were training the children to do only what they were told to do. That made it easier to handle a lot of children, but it took initiative away from them. Old Lafayette took the initiative away from his children; Rockefeller helped his develop initiative.

Elbert Hubbard observed that "the world reserves its big prizes for people who have initiative." These people are the self-starters. They don't need to have someone crank them up to get their motors running. Initiative is a superlative quality for personal leadership.

Some people have their initiatives undermined early in life, very early. Being weaned and changed from an easy liquid diet to a hard diet that needs chewing makes them feel cheated. As adults, they still want to live in a world of infantlike ease. They become the happy-go-lucky people, the initiative-lacking ne'er-do-wells. They feel the world owes them a living. They still have not been weaned.

These incompletely weaned folks are called "oral dependents" by the psychoanalysts. The oral dependents are human oysters at heart. You know how an oyster gets onward and upward in life. He rests on a comfortable bed at the bottom of a quiet cove. He does not show initiative, even to get food. He merely keeps his mouth open until the current washes some stray tidbits into his mouth. Mother Nature feeds him, and the ocean protects him.

And he shows no initiative even in his love life. If it were not for the friendly currents he would have no more progeny than a mule.

I have run across a good many human oysters who felt that things should come their way. They show no initiative in going out after responsibility. They wait for an opportunity to come to them, while the leader makes his opportunity. They think the boss owes them a raise, while the leader works for it. The world tends to be unkind to these human oysters, to say they are lazy, shiftless, lacking in ambition. But often they just have not been weaned from the childish attitude of oral dependence. Lafayette did not help his children wean themselves; he kept them dependent on him.

At times children have to take matters into their own hands if they are ever to be weaned from dependence on the family. Stephen Girard is one of the many who ran away from home to wean themselves. Others merely leave home, to go to school or to work in another town. This is a good sign for initiative.

Parents and bosses often conspire to beat the initiative

out of people, just as it has been trained out of most orphans.

Parents keep saying, "Ask me first."

Teachers keep saying, "Do as I tell you."

Then, when they go to work, the boss says to them:

"You do the work, I'll do the thinking," or, "I'm the one paid to make the decisions," or, "If your ideas were any good, the management would have thought of them years ago."

When initiative is smothered in this fashion, it makes people more like the laboratory trout than like oysters. Ordinarily a trout is a fighting fish, with initiative to burn. But in the laboratory, a way was found to take the initiative out of even a trout. The fish was placed in a rectangular tank. A plate-glass partition was placed in the middle, separating the tank into two compartments, with this invisible barrier between them. A nice juicy minnow was put in one compartment, opposite the trout.

Mr. Trout licked his chops. He was no oyster, waiting for the minnow to float into his mouth. He was a game fish, with initiative. He swished his tail and started for the minnow.

Bam! Mr. Trout's nose struck the glass plate. Perhaps he thought the minnow had swatted him on the nose. Mad now, he lunged again. But his nose whacked the glass partition again. He tried it several more times. Finally he gave up for the day, watching the minnow, but not trying to get it.

The next day, when the minnow was put in the other compartment to tempt the trout, he tried to get it again.

One day's bad luck had not eliminated all his initiative. But his heart was not in it.

The third day, he had still less interest in the minnow.

After a few more days the partition was removed, and the trout paid no attention to the minnow, even when it swam right past his nose. The trout's initiative had been so badly broken, in fact, that he stayed in his own end of the tank. He would swim up to where the glass partition used to be, flip his tail lifelessly, and turn around before he got another bump on his nose.

That invisible barrier took the initiative out of the trout.

A fish does not have many brains, to be sure. He did not discover what took away his initiative. Had he had brains enough he might have said something like this: "So, it has been that invisible barrier which broke me of the habit of using my initiative. Very well, then, I'll start practicing initiative. I'll start things, and finish them. I'll supervise myself and get back the initiative the barrier took out of me. They can't do this to me any longer!"

There is a new leading citizen in Lafayette's town today. When Lafayette was the first citizen, he used to buy his newspaper from a ragged but neat boy. He had his boots polished by the same boy on Saturday afternoons. The boy's father was dead; his mother and sister took in washings. His family was so poor that sometimes the patches on his trousers were themselves patched. But there were no patches on the seat of his trousers; he did not wear them out sitting around like an oyster.

Lafayette felt sorry for young Ralph. "Not much future for Ralph," townspeople said. Some of them thought it was terrible because his mother worked so hard at her steaming tubs that she could not boss him.

But folks should have envied Ralph. He was getting lots of practice in initiative. Ralph did not have many comforts; at times he even looked hungry. He could not be oral dependent. He had to use self-dependence.

There was no college for Ralph, of course, but he did work his way through a business school. That, too, took initiative.

After business school he started work, at the bottom of the ladder, in a small plant in his home town.

Ralph now owns the plant in which he started. He has another that he started on a shoestring. He is the most active person in the local government, the acknowledged leader in community enterprise.

Twenty-five years ago people felt sorry for him. They did not realize that he was getting the best education in the world. As soon as he was out of the high chair, fate enrolled him in the School of Initiative. He took course after course in self-dependence. He had to or starve.

I hope Ralph reads this chapter, and I rather think he will. When I last visited him he had just bought his children—two boys and a girl—a Shetland pony and cart. He showed me plans for the large house he expects to build on a conspicuous site, overlooking the golf course.

A cold dread gripped me as I looked at those elaborate plans. Across those blueprints stalked a vision of Lafayette's crumbled mansion, and I could imagine his initiative-starved children bobbing in and out of the underbrush. I wondered.

Would every half century see a repetition of the fate

of Lafayette's family? Does it have to be only two or
three generations from shirt sleeves to shirt sleeves?

In all our getting and all our giving, we must avoid
barriers to initiative.

Young Jim was cross-eyed. Life had not been too
happy for him for his first seventeen years, living with a
French family in bleak northern Scotland. Then he got
his hands on something that sharpened his initiative and
changed his life.

For two years he saved to run away. He landed at
Halifax, not yet twenty, and with only a dollar for each
year of his age. He did not have a solitary acquaintance
in this New World. He worked his way along the coast
to Portland, then to Boston, where he soon spent his last
penny and was without food for two days. No job could
be landed. The third day he had a stroke of luck; he
found a shilling on the Boston Common. Fortified at
last with food, he had more good luck and got a job, as
proofreader in a small print shop—just the sort of job he
wanted, too.

In a few years he had a series of personal failures to
his credit. He had tried to start a newspaper several
times, but things had turned sour. His initiative did not
turn sour, however, and he kept starting over. This time
he started in a damp basement, some boards placed between two barrels serving as his desk. Those barrels and
the planks atop them were the beginnings of the *New
York Herald*. James Gordon Bennett was still fighting
poverty, but his crossed eyes were still looking ahead to
his goal. He reached the goal in a big way.

The book he read at seventeen was Benjamin Franklin's "Autobiography." It sharpened his initiative to

strike out for himself. Oftentimes a book builds initiative when parents have lulled it into a semicomatose state.

Cecil Rhodes lacked tactfulness, but he became one of the world's outstanding leaders and empire builders. He lived his life backward. He was farming to get fresh air and sunshine for his tuberculosis when he was seventeen. He was a diamond digger in the newly found Kimberley fields at eighteen. In a year he was organizing claims, starting his firms, and was making half a thousand dollars a week. Then, at twenty, he quit all this feverish activity and went back to England to go to college, but he had difficulty getting them to let him enter.

Tactfulness he may have lacked, but he had initiative. And he had strong ideas about the initiative of others, too. "Give the children a sound education," he said, "and then kick all the props away. If they are worth anything the struggle will make them better men; if they are not, the sooner they go under the better for the world."

Later, when expanding the territories he controlled in South Africa, he had laws passed to levy fines on people who were lazy, who had their initiative in cold storage.

When someone lacks initiative, try building up his confidence in himself.

10

Five ways to build personal initiative

There is no shortage of opportunities; rather, there is a shortage of people who are wide-awake enough to jump into the opportunities. There are opportunities on every hand, literally millions of things that need to be done, waiting for leaders to start them.

The manager of a street railway noticed that the newly hired young man was picking up pieces of scrap iron around the yards in his spare moments. The lad had a neat scrap pile near the entrance to the car shops.

"What are you doing that for? Who told you to do that?"

"Why, no one told me. But someday these pieces of iron can be used."

Young Tom L. Johnson showed initiative. He became one of the country's outstanding traction magnates.

He didn't have to be shown an opportunity for work.

People with "go-ahead-itiveness" don't have to be shown. They go ahead on their own steam. They don't have to be led, for they become the leaders.

One exceptionally hot summer day I set out to buy a day bed for my study. I knew just what I wanted and I had the cash budget money in my pocket to pay for it. It was going to be an easy sale for some merchant.

Store number one was not busy. "Guess I can get

speedy service," I thought. There was only one customer on the floor and a salesman was in sight, too. He was sitting at a desk, writing. An oscillating fan was cooling him. He glanced at me but continued with his paper work while I wandered around and took inventory of what they had.

Shortly I became less interested in finding my spool-end day bed than in wondering how much profit there would be in the report he was writing. I started to approach him, but he only pulled his chair closer to the fan. Perhaps the store had just what I wanted, but I don't know. I didn't interrupt the salesman to find out.

Store number two had a giant fan to cool off the customers. A middle-aged salesman approached me. This was a good start. I explained what I wanted, and he showed me their stock of day beds. They did not have what I wanted, but he looked for it in a catalogue.

Did he have the catalogue of other manufacturers? Yes, but he did not know in which one to look. He had used all the initiative he had.

At the third store an alert high-school boy greeted me. It was his first week in the store, and he did not know much about their stock. "Let's look," he said with some initiative. They did not have what I wanted, so I suggested we look in catalogues. The boy asked the department manager about catalogues. The boy had initiative, but the manager let him down. The manager was quite certain I didn't know what I wanted. I really wanted one of the day beds they had.

Someone had to use initiative, so I came home and dropped a card to a former student, now in the furniture business halfway across the continent. I knew Bob used to have initiative. By return mail I had a letter from him, with a couple of pictures cut from catalogues. He would have what I wanted shipped immediately and directly to me.

Getting my day bed, after these barriers, is not the point of this series of experiences. It is an example of the widespread lack of initiative. Any one of the stores I visited could have made the sale with fifteen minutes of effort. But they could not break away from their routine, could not get more than a foot out of the rut.

This shopping experience is not exceptional, that is the tragedy of missing initiative.

Salesmen are not the only ones who lack needed initiative. Many physicians do not have enough initiative to keep up with new developments in medical science. Thousands of schoolteachers are in ruts. Many farmers barely make a living because they aren't self-starters. Office workers fail to get better jobs because they don't have the initiative to supervise themselves. Foremen remain little more than straw bosses because they need more initiative. Small businesses remain struggling because The Boss needs more initiative than he shows. And, according to Dorothy Dix, some men lack even the initiative to propose marriage.

Initiative gives one "git up and git." People who emerge from the crowd have it. It is another essential for leadership. Here are five aids for gaining this valuable characteristic for the leader's personality.

1. Be dissatisfied

A Chicago psychiatrist told me about a rich young man (like Lafayette's boys) whom he had been treating for abulia, or lack of will power, lack of initiative. Several months' treatment failed to help the young man. The specialist was almost ready to declare it hopeless.

Then the stock-market crash came. Overnight the inert fellow's wealth was wiped out. He moved from his bachelor penthouse into a hall bedroom.

For a few weeks he was dazed. His attitude was sullen. This attitude encouraged the specialist, for he felt it would make the young fellow dissatisfied. Slowly, the transformation came. His sullenness merged into determination.

He got himself a job and began to report for work at 8 A.M., earlier than he had risen in years. Then he started some night courses to help on his job. He helped other workers in the office, so that he could learn more about the business. He made several suggestions that the company adopted.

He got raises and promotions, each of which his reborn initiative justly earned for him. When the psychiatrist told me about this case, the young man had just been made a manager of one of the firm's branch offices.

The specialist frankly said that it was the stock crash, not the psychiatrist, that transformed the listless playboy into a Doer with initiative. It changed a Leaner into a Lifter. He had been too satisfied with himself and his lot in life. It took a major catastrophe to make a man out of him.

Thomas J. Watson is a Lifter with lots of initiative. He built the International Business Machines Corporation into one of the world's large corporations, with offices in every corner of the globe. He has accomplished this largely by using dissatisfaction. He made customers dissatisfied with the machines they had, so that they bought new ones. He made his research engineers dissatisfied with the machines the factory produced, so that they designed newer and better ones. He made his salesmen dissatisfied with their sales records, so that they upped their sales.

"When any individual, any industry, or any nation decides that it has arrived at success," Mr. Watson says, "that individual, or industry, or nation is headed the wrong way."

Charles M. Schwab started as a poor boy, working around the stables. In his prime of life he was earning a million dollars a year. He knew every luxury that money could buy and had an international fame that made him the companion of kings and presidents. Yet he kept on working, hard as ever.

Why didn't he quit and make room for some younger man? One day an interviewer asked the steel man if big businessmen ever reached their objectives.

"If a man ever reaches his objective," Schwab replied, "he is not a big businessman. It is ever onward, with successful men, until life flows out of their bodies."

If you are dissatisfied, count yourself lucky.

But if you are satisfied, better see a tombstone maker to have a marker chiseled for the grave of your initiative.

When the income-tax auditors were checking over the books of the L. M. N. Company they ran across a rather large annual bill from an expensive modiste shop in New York City. Why on earth would a brass-manufacturing concern have a legitimate expenditure in such an establishment?

The auditors smiled and disallowed it. "One of the brass hats is probably keeping a few glamour girls for his trips to New York," they commented, and spent a day looking for other expenses that might point in the same direction.

When the president saw the items the auditors had refused to deduct, he went through the ceiling.

"Hell's bells!" he exclaimed. "Those dresses are what make our sales volume climb. I buy expensive dresses for the wives of our division managers, better dresses than the girls ever owned. That makes them dissatisfied with the ready-mades in their neighborhood shops, and they keep after the boys to bring home more commissions so that they can keep wearing dresses like those."

No scandal at all. The expense was allowed.

If your wife keeps after you to accomplish more, thank the little lady.

If your boss thinks you could do better, he may be keeping you from dying on your feet.

2. Change your wishbone for a backbone

An ancient Chinese proverb says, "Great souls have wills, feeble ones have only wishes."

Dissatisfaction does not help initiative unless one uses one's backbone. Wishing makes one an idle dreamer. Putting backbone into the wish makes the Doer.

I have talked with many people who thought they were ambitious. One was dissatisfied with his poor education and complained that he did not have more. He had done nothing about it, however. He had not attended night-school courses or taken a correspondence course. He had wishbone, no backbone.

Another wished to become a famous musician. He played well enough, considering the little practice he made himself do. All he got from his playing was free meals in a beer parlor. He wished he was famous but lacked the backbone to train himself.

Many have wished to become managers but have done nothing to prepare themselves for the responsible jobs, except to complain about the boss and wish they had his job.

Such people are not really ambitious. They have an itch around the wishbone that they misinterpret as ambition. This is usually worse during the high-school age; it is one of the things that makes handling young people a problem. By the time they reach the mature age of twenty-five many have outgrown this wishbone itch, but those who lack initiative may have the itch all through life.

Back in 1891 a boy was born to a poor family in Bolshoye Bikovo, Russia. When he was fourteen—the wishbone age—he came to this country with his mother. Soon he found himself on a rundown farm in central New York State, working from sunup until after sundown on the unprofitable land. He was glad to be in this country but dissatisfied with his lot as a farm laborer. He could have stayed in Russia and had the same job.

He wanted something better, something in which he could express himself. But Maurice Gerschon Hindus had a backbone, not a wishbone. He heard of a college some miles away and applied for admission.

The professors would not accept him as a student, since he did not have a high-school education. One professor, however, was favorably impressed by the boy's initiative and backbone. This professor talked the others into giving the dissatisfied boy a chance to show whether he could do college work.

So Maurice Hindus started college that fall. It was not easy, for he had to make up many high-school courses in addition. He also had to continue to work on the farm.

Now he got up before daybreak to get the farm chores done before his five-mile walk to college. He studied as he walked. Back at the farm after the day's classes, he had to pitch into farm work again. He studied as he milked the cows.

Dr. Maurice Hindus is now a world-famous American writer and lecturer on Russian affairs. His books have been bestsellers. The college that almost didn't admit him has honored him with advanced degrees.

He would still be a fatigued farmhand, milking cows and ploughing unproductive, quack-grass-infested soil, if his dissatisfaction had only made him wishful. But he had the backbone to build his career, not dream about it.

Wishes must be put into action, by expressing them through the backbone.

3. *Think positively*

"Maybe I can" marks the beginning of a crumbled initiative.

"I'd like to, but it may be too difficult," is part of the odor given off by a rotting initiative.

Folk who have let their initiatives wither tend to think up reasons why they should not do things. They keep saying "no" to their goals.

An extreme example of this was the white-trash southern farmer. He didn't plant cotton because he was afraid the boll weevil would get it. He gave up the idea of planting potatoes, since potato bugs might get them. So he played safe and planted nothing.

Thousands think in such negative, discouraging ways. Naturally they are not self-starters; they have well-exercised brakes that keep them stalled most of the time.

Thinking on the red side of the ledger of life gets nothing started, nothing done.

It is told that in the First World War a lieutenant was ordered to execute a hazardous foray. In a few hours the lieutenant came back to tell the general many reasons why the expedition should not be undertaken.

"Every reason you have given is plausible," the general told him. "Now, go ahead and do it!"

Many people have found they can reverse this tendency to negative thinking. When they begin to wonder if they should do something, they write down all the reasons why they should not do it. Then they seal this list in an envelope and drop it in the wastebasket. Then they do it.

Most of our alleged reasons for not doing things are merely flimsy excuses, alibis. People with weak initiatives have this self-alibi habit. Writing the "excuses" on the paper is easy for them, and gets the negative approach out of the system.

Those who have the tendency to think of alibis, rather than doing things, give this tendency away by such expressions as:

"Yes, but . . ."

"On the other hand . . ."

"Let's wait and see what happens."

Those phrases help put initiative in a wheel chair.

Alice MacDougall had led a comfortable life. She was happy with her growing family. Then her husband began to act queerly. A complete breakdown overtook him. Her once comfortable life became a nightmare. Resources dwindled. She had to go on charity or make a living.

There was go-ahead-itiveness in Alice Foote MacDougall's nature. She started in business for herself, in the only business she knew anything about—coffee—and she had to learn a lot more about it. She started on a miserably tiny scale but did manage to make expenses for her little family.

Slowly, almost imperceptibly at times, she made the business grow. Others advised her against little expansions, but she went ahead on her own initiative. She started a little coffee shop in Grand Central Terminal, and it was almost a dead loss. She held on to it, put more effort into it. At last it turned the corner.

She started a larger coffee shop, then another.

Her go-ahead-itiveness built up a million-dollar business. She thought positively.

"I simply don't believe in failure," she said. "We create it. We make ourselves fail. Conditions present obstacles, of course, but there is a way to overcome them. In itself, failure doesn't exist."

Harvey was an Ohio farm boy who did not think in terms of self-alibis. His initiative was not in a wheel chair. When he had saved a thousand dollars as a buggy salesman, he located a partner who had half that much capital. Together they started a rubber factory in Chicago. They planned to make rubber tires for buggies, but competitors kept them from using a necessary patented machine.

Harvey's life savings were at stake. They had not made a single tire. Did he think of all the reasons why he should give up and return to selling buggies? Not Harvey S. Firestone. He got a mechanic, and together they experimented. By using his initiative, he found a better and cheaper way to make the tires, without using the patented machine. He became independent of the patent monopoly because *he thought positively.*

When he was thirty-one he sold his interest in the buggy-tire factory for $45,000 and looked for other places to use his initiative. A gangling young friend who worked for the electric company in Detroit was working on a mechanical buggy in his spare time. Harvey Firestone thought that there might be a future to this horseless buggy Henry Ford was developing.

In those days the woods were full of doubters who could only see why a horseless buggy would be no good. But Firestone and Ford were thinking positively.

So Firestone took his $45,000, his family, and his initiative to Akron and started to make hollow, inflated tires for those new horseless carriages. He bought a tumble-down foundry for a factory, a near-by shed for his office, and an assortment of secondhand machinery that the former owners had thought was on the red side of the ledger.

Again a patent monopoly kept him from making tires of the then popular "clincher" type. It looked as if he might have to close down and let his twelve workmen go. But he thought positively. A barrier was not going to lick him.

He developed the straight-side tire himself and patented it.

He visited Henry Ford in 1905 and conveyed his positive thinking about the merits of a straight-side tire to Ford. Firestone returned to Akron with an order for 2,000 sets of his new kind of tire.

What is a monopoly against initiative like that!

The bigger the monopoly, the harder they fell for Firestone. At the close of the First World War, for instance, he ran into foreign government monopolies on the supply of crude rubber. He immediately sent his own engineering and exploring parties around the globe. Behind a wall of jungle that seemed impenetrable, he established his own rubber plantations in Liberia. His own fighting initiative and positive thinking brought independence to the rubber industry.

He did pretty well for a young fellow starting out for himself with only a thousand dollars. His real asset, however, was worth millions more. That was the positive thinking of initiative.

He was not in the excuse business.

He thought about how things could be done, not about why they should not be.

4. Take on more work

The less people have to do, the harder it is for them to do it.

The less people have to start themselves, the harder it is for them to start.

The world owes a lot to young men who took on more work, of their own free will. For instance:

That young engineer in Detroit who worked nights, on his own time, to build the first automobile for the common people, Henry Ford.

Yeah!!

But...

DID YOU GET THE BUSINESS?

Alibi-puncturing cartoon which reminds sales and advertising representatives that their job is getting business, not explaining why they didn't get it.

This is given to their field forces by the Meredith Publishing Co.

That young teacher in Massachusetts who worked after school, on his own time, to develop the first telephone, Alexander Graham Bell.

That young bank clerk in Rochester who worked after hours, on his own initiative, to devise a new kind of dry plate for cameras, George Eastman.

Most employees, I am afraid, hesitate to do any more work than the company pays them for. They don't realize that, as they do more work, they are likely to be doing it for themselves, rather than for the company. A young immigrant from Sweden realized this. He got a job, when he was eighteen, as tariff clerk for the Great Northern Railroad. He was paid $50 a month. But he earned much more than that—for himself.

In eight years he was head of the department. He became the department chief because, as soon as he had finished the work for which he was being paid, he helped some of the other clerks with their work.

The others were glad to have someone help them, especially anyone who was sap enough to do it without getting extra pay. And night after night, too, Bror Gustave Dahlberg returned to the office to do some other fellow's work. He earned nothing immediately from this, but he learned so much about the department that he became chief at twenty-six years of age.

He had initiative. It became stronger as he took on extra work.

It became so strong that soon he set himself up as a consultant on tariff problems.

Then his initiative took him into paper manufacturing, then into making building boards. Today we can thank Bror G. Dahlberg because our homes are cooler in summer and warmer in winter. It was his initiative that put across home insulation.

Had he attended to his own job and no more, he would perhaps today be a pensioner of the Great Northern. Instead, he is president of the Celotex Corporation and director of several other organizations that he built through his initiative. He kept his initiative alive and growing by taking on more work than he needed to do for his pay check.

Welcome committee work, extra opportunities, outside activities, more work. They may interfere with your wishful thinking but will force you to keep the habit of doing things.

5. Wean yourself

Personal comfort, pleasure, play, ease, are the deciding motives for some people. As we found in the preceding chapter, these folk have not weaned themselves from the dependent attitude of childhood. Although such people gravitate toward the easy side of life, they are likely to be cantankerous rather than cheery. They don't see why they should take on more work. They would rather use their wishbones than their backbones.

They still have the childish notion that others should take care of them. They wait until the last minute before getting out of a comfortable bed mornings and lament because they were not born rich and have to work. They spend money for goodies and recreation, little for books or magazines on their work. They are self-starters only when it is for a chance to play.

Some of these folk who need weaning can blame their parents because they did not let the young persons manage themselves in childhood.

Animals seem, at times, to have better sense in this than humans. Every spring I watch a nest of birds just outside the study window. As soon as the young birds are large enough, the mother forcefully shoves them out of their cosy nest. She starts their weaning. After much scolding, they always manage to fly back to the nest.

After a few more days, she does not let them return to the nest. They have to look for their own food.

On the other hand, some animals (including humans) are so dependent that they refuse to be weaned, except by drastic actions.

Some calves, for instance, are so stubborn about staying dependent that they will steal milk from all the cows in the pasture. It is a ludicrous sight to see a full-grown steer down on his knees, his neck bent uncomfortably, nursing away and wagging his tail in dependent contentment.

Farmers have a drastic remedy for these cattle that hate to be weaned. A wire muzzle, with sharp projecting prongs, is strapped to his snout. When he tries to drink in some of the easy goods the world owes him, he gets a sharp kick in the face from the cow who was stuck by those prongs. That helps wean him.

Adult humans who are not weaned get a good many kicks in the face, too. The world may give them a living, but it does not give them positions of leadership.

For INITIATIVE to GET THINGS GOING

Be dissatisfied
Change your wishbone for a backbone
Think positively
Take on more work
Wean yourself

11

The vital three feet to achievement

For many years I have kept a magic rule on my desk. It has literally been worth more than its weight in gold to me. When I have an impulse to quit, this rule keeps me at work. When I become discouraged, it whispers encouragement. When I stop too long to watch the river, the rule calls me back.

It all started back in the Colorado gold rush. A small-town Marylander was bit by the gold bug. This young man made the long trip to Colorado and started to dig for his fortune.

And he did strike gold—an unusually rich vein. His find was so large that pick-and-shovel digging was inadequate. He needed machinery.

He hurried back to Maryland, breathlessly told friends of his gold strike, of the great opportunity, and of the need for money to install machinery. He took their money back to Colorado, and soon the machines were loosening the richest ore yet discovered.

Then one day the ore suddenly failed. The new machines were bringing out just plain dirt. So the mine was sold to a dealer in secondhand machinery, and the disillusioned prospectors returned to Maryland and their debtors.

The secondhand-machinery man left the machines intact and called in some experts who understood the peculiarities of the mountains. They examined the property and discovered that, centuries before, the crust of the earth had slipped at the very spot where the disappointed easterners halted digging. Dig a little more, the experts said, and you will pick up the vein of ore again.

The new owner started the machinery and dug one foot, two feet, three feet, and, lo! there was the rich ore again. If the original owners had only stuck to it for three more feet!

The original owner was made bankrupt by the mine, but it also made him rich. It made him rich by the lesson it taught—to stick to it, not to quit at the first discouragement. Those three vital feet that he neglected to dig in Colorado haunted him.

Back east, he became a salesman. Those three vital feet made him a star salesman. When he was given "no" as an answer, he would come back to the prospect later and dig another foot, then another, and usually made a sale.

By digging those vital three feet he made enough money as one of the country's outstanding salesmen to pay off all those friends who had sunk money in the Colorado mine.

To remind me of the story of the vital three feet, I bought a three-foot folding rule back in 1920. It has been doing magic for me ever since. Here is how it first worked.

I wrote a paper for one of my courses and thought it was so important that it should be published. But I didn't have nerve enough to submit it to a good magazine. I mailed it to the sorriest-looking magazine I could locate, and waited. I didn't have to wait long; it came back by return mail and with an uncomplimentary remark written on it.

Maybe the article wasn't so good, after all. If that was what a poor editor thought, what would a good one think? I was ready to quit authoring and return to working with the insane. Apparently I got along better with them than with editors.

Then that three-foot folding rule looked at me. It said, "Dig some more!"

I retyped the article and mailed it to another magazine, which seemed to publish almost anything. When it came back promptly, with two strikes on it, I again almost gave up the idea. But I hadn't counted on that three-foot rule; it made me send it out again and again.

One magazine kept it a long while, and I began buying copies of the magazine each week to see the article when it appeared in print. Then I got a letter returning the manuscript, which had been misplaced.

There was finally only one magazine left on my list. It was the one of which I was most afraid. And I would never have sent the manuscript if that three-foot rule hadn't said, "Go on, you've only dug two feet and ten inches so far."

It was not returned promptly. Misplaced again, I thought. And when I saw a small envelope from the *Yale Review* one morning I was sure the manuscript had been lost. I tell you it was hard work to open that blue envelope.

It was from Dean Wilbur Cross himself. He liked the article and wondered if I would consider $35 adequate payment.

I felt like kissing that folding rule, until I figured up how much I had paid for postage and retyping during the two years the article was riding in mail cars. I still figure I lost money on it, but I won the lesson of the three vital feet.

A good many thousand people have heard the story of the magic ruler that keeps people continually achieving. It has given new determination to many. I once told the story at a high-school commencement. Six months later a woman introduced herself to me and thanked me for what the story had meant to her daughter, who had been in the graduating class. The girl had left home to work in a strange city. She was plagued by homesickness for the first few weeks but stuck to her job when she remembered the story of the ruler. She tried to buy a three-foot folding rule but could find none. A young hardware clerk offered to break a six-foot rule in half for her, if she would tell him why she wanted one only three feet long.

She told him, and he kept the other half for himself.

"You know," her enthusiastic mother continued, "now they are engaged! He used his half to make him keep at it, too!"

And I might have told the mother that the principal of that school placed an ordinary yardstick on his own desk. His wife was passing through a particularly trying time, and he had been on the verge of seeking a separation. The yardstick gave him just the touch of silent counsel he needed to stick it out.

So often people fail to achieve what they might because they stop only a foot or two short of triumph.

The three-foot rule helps them down the last few hard inches that pay off. It reminds them to keep digging.

Be sure you are wrong before you quit.

Keeping at it gives people a touch of genius. The famous studies of geniuses made by Stanford University show that persistence is their outstanding characteristic— not stubbornness, but doggedly working at it despite rebuffs or bad luck.

Cyrus McCormick had it, but other men of his day who invented a reaper lacked it. The hand harvesting of grain was wasteful and backbreaking, yet farmers would not buy the reapers. Maybe they were tradition-bound and in ruts, for getting them to use the reaper was more of a job than inventing it. McCormick might have stopped after trying the first year. Others had stopped. But McCormick kept at it two, three, five, ten years, and, in seventeen years he had sold one hundred reapers! It takes persistence to overcome the resistance of others. McCormick had that touch of genius, stick-to-itiveness.

Edison had it. He tried 6,000 substances before he found the right one for the filament in his early electric light. He tried 28,000 things to find a substitute for lead in storage batteries. Edison's own comment was, "Nearly every man who develops an idea works it up to the point where it looks impossible, and then becomes discouraged. That's the time to become interested!"

Robert E. Peary tried seven times to reach the North Pole and failed each time, but he learned something from each failure. After keeping at it for twenty-three years, he planted the Stars and Stripes on the Pole on his eighth try. Lying helpless on the Arctic wastes, both feet badly ulcerated from frostbite, he wrote, "I will find a way, or make one." Stick-to-itiveness!

Museums and collectors the world over prize that superb pottery which is known as Plaissy ware. These pieces were made in the 1500's by a Frenchman who would not give up. No enameled pottery was then made in France; its manufacture was a secret kept by the Moors and Italians. Bernard Plaissy used up his meager resources, his credit, his townspeople's patience, trying for years to find how to put a glaze on pottery. His furniture was sold or burned in his kiln. He tore up his fence to get fuel for another experiment in his kiln. This went on for sixteen years. But he finally found the secret of making the lustrous white enamel. Those museum pieces are today worth their weight in gold. Whenever you look at a china cup or dish, remember the story of Plaissy's stick-to-itiveness, which enabled him to rediscover the secret of the glaze, and live with royalty. Even a cheap teacup can teach the leader.

Paul Ehrlich tried 605 remedies for syphilis. He received the Nobel prize for his success on the six hundred and sixth try.

Charles Darwin worked on his studies of evolution for twenty years, though racked with pain much of the time. "It's doggedness that does it," he said.

Frank Woolworth's first four stores were complete failures. But he kept at the idea, changing it slightly as he learned from the failures. Think of that when you stop in one of his stores to buy a folding rule.

George H. Bucher kept after the Westinghouse Electric & Manufacturing Co. for three months before he could get a job with them. When he was forty-eight years old he was president of the company.

Charles Goodyear spent more than five years, half starving, sick, dodging debtors' prison, laughed at, working on a way to cure or vulcanize rubber.

A thousand independent automobile makers have failed and been forgotten. Henry Ford was on the brink of failure twice. Once, racked with illness, momentarily discouraged, he nearly quit. But he could find no banker who thought his business was worth buying. That was his good luck, for he stuck by the ship and brought it into port with a cargo richer than any of the bankers' dreams.

The great Pasteur, also, almost quit. In the midst of his work he was struck down with paralysis. The entire nation watched his progress. The government, which was building a special laboratory for his work, halted construction pending good news from his physicians. His recovery was slow. There were long days of inactivity, weakness, helplessness . . . brooding.

Pasteur was giving up! What can we do to get him to want to get well, to finish his important work? the physicians asked. Then someone gave him a simple little book. It had been translated from English. "Self-help" was its title. It was a homage to will power, illustrated by the lives of famous men.

"I must get well," he said. "I *will* get well and find the cause of that silkworm disease."

There were tears of joy in his physicians' eyes. A few weeks later there were shouts of praise on the lips of thousands of his countrymen. For the great Pasteur, though not fully recovered, had discovered the cause of the plague in their silk-producing districts. That little book, "Self-help," renewed his stick-to-itiveness. I have tried dozens of old bookstores to find a copy of this book by Dr. Smiles but have not succeeded. In the meantime, I am content with my own folding three-foot rule for keeping me everlastingly at it.

Herbert Fleishhacker, financial genius who led the development of southern California, went to work when he was fourteen. "I gained the most valuable experience as a drummer on the road for seven years, starting when I was seventeen," he comments. "There I learned the necessity for stick-to-itiveness. They simply couldn't discourage me. If they kicked me out the front door, I returned, smiling, at the back door. I called on some prospects regularly for three or four years before I finally landed them."

A rough farm boy who left more than a hundred million dollars and a great university was himself uneducated and admitted—perhaps honestly—that he had only fair ability. "I guess the reason I have succeeded in business," Buck Duke observed, "is because I have stuck to it longer. I know plenty of people who have failed in everything, and they were a lot smarter than I am, but they lacked determination."

And listen to the self-made man, John Wanamaker: "As I grow older it becomes clear that the difference between men who accomplish things and those who fail is in correct thinking, energy, and invincible determination. A single aim and a strong spirit, undistracted and untiring, seldom fall short of the goal. The man who never quits until the work is done inevitably writes his name on the roll of winners."

Daniel Willard's first job was shoveling manure, at 10 cents an hour. His next job was as a railroad section hand, at 9 cents an hour. When he was vice-president of the Burlington railroad a crew was drilling for water at Edgemont, S. D. They failed to find water and recommended quitting. Thirty thousand dollars had already been spent on what seemed to be a dry hole in the earth.

"Go on with the drilling," Willard told them.

Within a week they struck a plentiful flow of artesian water.

It was many years later, in the depression of the 1930's, that this well-drilling experience saved all the railroads, and railroad workers, from a crisis that seemed unavoidable. The railroads were on the brink of bankruptcy, and wages had to be reduced. Single-handed, Willard brought railroad and union officers together.

Hundreds gathered in Chicago, and the nation waited for the momentous decision from this conference. After twenty days of discussion and wrangling they seemed no closer together. All participants were tired, many irritated, and growing numbers were discouraged and ready to give up. Willard himself had a flicker of discouragement. Then he recalled that well in South Dakota. He kept the discussions going, and on the twenty-first day men and management reached an agreement. Just one day longer!

Mrs. Henry Breckenridge was losing her eyesight. A young physician and surgeon, Dr. William H. Wilmer, saved it for her. Her gratitude knew no bounds, and she set out to raise funds for a laboratory and research center for work on diseases of the eye. A Rockefeller agent promised her a million dollars, provided that she could get Johns Hopkins University to raise another million and her own friends a third million.

J. P. Morgan promised Mrs. Breckenridge $10,000 toward her million dollars. Then Dr. William H. Welch went to New York to call on Mr. Morgan. The ruddy doctor talked with quiet enthusiasm about medical research at Johns Hopkins.

"I'll raise that to $25,000," Mr. Morgan told him.

The medical director nodded and kept on talking.

"Well, I'll make it $50,000."

Dr. Welch nodded again, kept on talking.

"$75,000."

Dr. Welch kept right on talking.

"$100,000—and not a cent more."

"The funny thing about it," Dr. Welch said afterward, "was that I never asked Mr. Morgan for one penny!"

But it was just such stick-to-itiveness that helped establish the world-famed Wilmer Ophthalmology Pavilion at Johns Hopkins University.

Sometimes a wife can give a man the stick-to-itiveness he needs when the road becomes rough or events discouraging.

When he had nothing to lose and everything to gain, McCormick had stick-to-itiveness. Then, in 1871, the Chicago fire reduced his two-million-dollar plant to ashes. Wearing his half-burned overcoat, McCormick went to the smoking ruins with his young wife. It was a discouraging scene. But McCormick was a rich man now and could easily retire and live on his other investments. He was going to quit the reaper business.

"No, no, go on," his wife pleaded with him, holding his arm more tightly.

"All right, Nettie, we'll stay in the reaper business if

you insist." And to the anxious men who were watching the ruins, he shouted in his shrill voice, "We're going to rebuild!"

In three months they were again making farm reapers.

Then there was Potter Palmer. His fortune was mostly in Chicago real estate. He had been married the very year of the great fire, to a dashing Kentucky girl half his age. He had planned to retire, but the fire had wiped out nine-tenths of his holdings. Well, he could still retire, and he would, for he was disheartened.

In his low voice he told pretty Bertha that he would let others assume the risks of rebuilding Chicago, the city he had helped build.

"Mr. Palmer," Bertha Honore Palmer flashed back at him, "it's the duty of every Chicagoan to stay here and help rebuild this stricken city." He stayed, and built.

When the digging gets hard, many look for an excuse to quit. That is the very time when the wise person digs all the harder.

When diamonds were first discovered in the rich Kimberley fields, Dutch, English, and native Kaffirs started digging, excitedly but easily. The diamonds were found in an undreamed-of abundance, in softish yellow ground. It was easy digging, with rich rewards. Men were making hundreds of dollars a day, in their little claims thirty-one feet square.

But the soft yellow earth was finally all removed. The diamond diggers came to a layer of blue dirt. Their shovels scarcely scratched this blue earth, it was so hard.

"Well," they said to each other, "the diamonds must all have been in the yellow ground that was so easy to shovel. The pay dirt must be gone."

So a young Englishman, who had gone to South Africa to cure his tuberculosis, walked through their tiny claims and bought out the miners who didn't like to work the tough blue stratum. He got their claims for small sums, and for these small sums he got the richest diamond deposits in all the world, for the real deposits of diamonds were in that blue dirt which was so hard to work.

When that Englishman died at forty-eight, still a young man, he left behind an enormous fortune of more than thirty millions of dollars. Cecil Rhodes dug in when the digging got too hard for others.

When you feel like quitting, let a three-foot rule give you a rap on the knuckles and knuckle down to finish the job!

Leadership is attained by sustained action.

(Shortly after the publication of this book we became indebted to S. L. Myer, of Warren, Pa., and Elias Oddstad, of Seattle, Wash., for locating copies of "Self-help" by Dr. Samuel Smiles—the book that gave Pasteur stick-to-itiveness.)

12

How to get stick-to-itiveness

Metallurgists had developed a new, tough steel with unusual properties. Production executives tried it and reported it could not be used in manufacture, because it was too hard to be worked. They had tried to drill it, but the drills bent without even scratching the surface.

"Don't blame the steel," Charles F. Kettering told them. "It's not too hard. Your drills are too soft." And, using a diamond-pointed drill, they quickly bored into the new steel.

Dr. Kettering told this incident at a meeting of the United States Chamber of Commerce to show that usually the job is not too hard but that the men may be too soft. They need to harden their cutting edges with some stick-to-itiveness.

The scene shifts to a quiet club in New York City. A group of top-flight leaders of American business are discussing the serious shortage of men who are capable of taking executive responsibility. There are plenty of men with sufficient intelligence and knowledge of the businesses, they agree, but these men fail to meet two requirements. The difficulty is to find men who can be trusted to keep confidences and men who have shown they have determination, doggedness, persistence—in short, stick-to-itiveness.

There are lots of Jacks-of-all-trades, men who know a little about this and that, but there is a shortage of men who have stuck to any one thing long enough to have mastered it before shifting to something more glamorous. Too many change jobs when they should stick to the old one a bit longer. They give up when they should push on. They start more things than they finish.

You as a leader cannot waver, cannot be unsteady. There are five things that help make you stand firmly, continue steadfastly.

1. *Sink your ships*

People stick to their tasks when they know they cannot retreat. That is what won the liberation of Texas.

The enemy had taken the Alamo, a frightful massacre. Then their trained and well-equipped soldiers stalked the Texas volunteers for weeks. Samuel Houston led his army of 800 grumbling volunteers backward, always backward. Heavy rains came, but the retreat went on through the mud. The grumblings increased. As the Lone Star army was on the verge of open revolt, they came face to face with the enemy at San Jacinto.

The dispirited 800 Texans at last faced a force of 1,600 of the enemy.

And reinforcements were coming to the enemy! General Houston sent a frontier character, Erastus Smith, to cut a bridge over which the enemy reinforcements would have to travel. Smith was known as Deaf Smith, from a defect in hearing, and a Texas county is today named Deaf Smith in his honor.

Unknown to the Texas forces, Deaf Smith galloped off with axes to cut the bridge.

As Houston rode in front of his line, a Mexican bugle sounded in the enemy camp, and muskets spit orange fire at the Texans. The white stallion fell from under Houston, and he jumped on a cavalryman's pony.

"Hold your fire, men!" he shouted. But a few Texans fired back. "Damn you, hold your fire!" And Houston resumed his patrol of the harried lines.

A lathered mustang snorted up the plains. It was Deaf Smith returning.

"Fight for your lives!" Deaf Smith shouted in a voice like a cuckoo clock. "Vince's bridge has been cut down!"

The Texans mistakenly thought that this was a bridge that would make their retreat impossible.

Houston signaled his frightened men with his hat. "Remember the Alamo! Remember the Alamo!" he cried. The Texans took up his cry and dashed forth.

At sunset Houston fainted; his ankle was shattered and he had lost a bootful of blood. There had been only six Texans killed, twenty-four wounded.

The battle itself lasted less than half an hour, which shows the fury of men who think their retreat is gone. Houston's handful of men, thinking their backs to the wall, had killed 630 of the enemy, wounded 208, and taken 730 prisoners.

And one of their prisoners was Antonio López de Santa Anna, commander in chief and president of Mexico.

Every schoolboy knows about the battle cry, "Remember the Alamo!"

But there is a real lesson for leadership—of oneself and of others—in the high-pitched cry of Deaf Smith: "Vince's bridge has been cut down!"

Cutting the bridge did keep Santa Anna's reinforcements from reaching his main army in time. But more than that, the Texans' misunderstanding of the news instantly gave them the desperation of a singleness of purpose.

Cutting bridges makes history by forcing greater determination.

Hernando Cortes set out to capture the fabulous kingdom of Montezuma, in Mexico. Cortes sailed from Cuba with a handful of only 618 men. They landed in 1519 and started the city of Vera Cruz, and he burned his ships, leaving his tiny army marooned in hostile country. It was glory or death for them. They won the glory.

Burning the bridges or sinking the ships is nothing new, but individuals often neglect to do this.

Julius Caesar saw to it that his soldiers stuck to their jobs. As soon as the equipment was unloaded from the galleys, he had the ships burned and sunk offshore, in full view of the startled warriors. There would be no retreating for them, no ships in which to get away when the fighting got tough. They had to stick to it—or else.

Many people help their stick-to-itiveness by, figuratively, sinking their ships. They deliberately make it impossible for themselves to quit.

One automobile agent in the Northwest, for instance, ordered a whole trainload of automobiles from the factory. In past years he had sold only a fraction of this number. He only had enough finances to take the automobiles a carload at a time. But he worked like never before to sell the first load, then rushed with the money to release the next carload. He sold all the automobiles, because he had to. He knew how disastrous it would be if he quit.

Wise managers set quotas that strike their men as impossible, yet the men crash through and do the impossible, time and time again. A "reasonable" quota or goal does not encourage stick-to-itiveness.

A young self-made man suddenly found himself in the president's chair of one of our largest advertising agencies. He was determined to make a success of the job, so he departed from the usual policy of deep secrecy about plans. He told people what he was going to do for the business. They thought he was bragging, but he wasn't. He was sinking his ships. He told them so that, when the going got hard and he might be tempted to quit, he would have to eat his own words.

That was not the first time that he had sunk his ships and got results. He had been a heavy smoker, had tried to quit several times, but always slid back into his chain-smoking habits. But when he told several associates that he had quit, then he did not dare to smoke. He has not smoked since that morning.

By sinking his ships, he made retreat more unpleasant than fighting through to a winning conclusion. Sticking was less embarrassing than quitting would have been.

Tenacity of purpose is helped by knowing that one has to live up to something.

That is what Martin Luther did. It kept him steadfast in his religious reformation of old Germany. He wrote out his convictions in a bold hand and nailed them fast to the cathedral door, where all could see them. It was then impossible for him to compromise with himself or to back water when his tormentors got after him. He sank his ships and became the religious leader of his people.

Tell the world in advance, or, at least, tell someone who will know and disapprove if you don't stick to it.

Cut off your retreat. Then it is either sink or swim. And you'll swim.

2. *Change your grip, not your goal*

Discouragement is a natural enemy of stick-to-itive-ness. Yet discouraging situations are inevitable. Progress toward a goal is never uniform. Some days we spurt; then may come a disappointing week when no progress is made. This is what psychologists call the "plateau of despond."

These plateaus of despond were first discovered in experiments with persons learning telegraphy. Each learner had periods when, practice as he would, he could not improve either speed or accuracy. After a week or so on this discouraging plateau, Eureka! suddenly he would begin to gain. And there are plateaus of despond for practically every human activity.

These plateaus make many folk give up. A business-man came to me a short while ago. He had started an undertaking that had gone well enough for a while, then seemed to slump. He was ready to quit, lose his invest-ment, and start over again at something else. I knew that he was an ardent golfer and that he had threatened to quit the game a few months before because he couldn't improve his score. He was at a plateau in his golf then, just as he now was in his business. Friends had talked him into having a golf professional coach him, rather than quit the game.

The professional showed him how to make a slight change in the way he gripped the clubs. This change bettered his score by nearly ten points. He was elated with the results, remained an enthusiastic golfer. He did not quit the game; he merely changed his grip.

I reminded him of his golf experience, and he quickly saw the similarity with his present business predicament. So we looked for ways to change the approach, the grip on his business. He did not look for a new business to enter after he liquidated the present one.

He stuck to it, with a slight change in method, and it brought results.

When people hit this plateau of despond they often have the inclination to quit entirely. But a slight change in minor things—plus a lot of determination—will usually bridge the plateau quickly.

We learned earlier about McCormick's stick-to-itiveness in promoting his reaper. He did not keep stubbornly at it along the same lines. His approach, his grip, was continually changing. In devising new approaches he pioneered in many business innovations that are now commonplace. Farmers were skeptical, for instance, so he originated a written guarantee, "warranting the performance of the reaper in every respect." This change of grip meant seven sales that year.

In 1848 he introduced a free trial and partial payments. He was reckless enough to announce a standard price, when the practice at the time was to get all the trade could stand. He appointed responsible local men as branch distributors; in 1849 he had nineteen of these, although only seven machines had been sold the year before.

Each of these schemes was an innovation for that era. He was trying anything that might break the log jam. The thirty or so other reaper inventors did not change their grip. They fought along the same old lines—and soon had to stop the fight.

"When you find yourself working hard and accomplishing little, stop for a space and analyze yourself," was the advice of Harvey Firestone. "True self-analysis is a great accomplishment. It is the only means that will lead you to profit by experience."

That is changing the grip, not blindly, but on the basis of analysis.

It works in family relations, too. A thirty-year-old woman, mother of two lovely children, was going to leave her husband. Her husband, poor soul, did not suspect it, and I doubt if he will ever know how close he was to being a grass widower. His wife had no complaint about him.

It was his mother, who lived with them, who was unbearable to the younger woman. She knew her husband would not put his mother out, and she could no longer stand having her mother-in-law tell her how to prepare meals, bake good old-fashioned pies, use a broom instead of a vacuum cleaner, and dozens of other picayune interferences.

Why not try a different approach, a new grip before quitting? Old folk love to relive the old days, to regress. Why not encourage the older woman to entertain her grandchildren with stories of how she used to bake Boston brown bread and molasses cookies in a hard-to-regulate Dutch oven, how she saved ashes to make soap, how she went to bed on cold nights with heated bricks to keep her feet warm?

The young wife tried that change in grip. Her mother-in-law became so engrossed in recollections for the grandchildren that she neglected to criticize can-opener housekeeping. The children were enthralled. The lad actually started to wash behind his ears, because grandmother told him about a great-uncle, captain in the War between the States, who always washed behind his ears and often had to use icy water. One day the boy put ice cubes in his wash water!

How about the young woman who was on the brink of quitting? She is happy as a lark but is provoked at herself for ever thinking of walking out.

When the veil of discouragement descends or when results seem to taper off, that is the time to look for slight changes, to alter the grip, not to quit. That is the time to make a fresh start, but in a slightly different way. Keep the goal; merely change the approach slightly.

Despond yields only dross. Keeping at it yields gold.

3. Say "no" to yourself

There are two D's which undermine persistence.

One is Discouragement.

The other is Distraction.

This rule, to say "no" to yourself, is especially useful for those who are diverted into desultory devices by distractions.

These folk are the butterflies. They waver from one attractive flower to another. Butterflies go in a zigzag course, haphazardly. Bees stick to one flower until the nectar is extracted.

Human butterflies zigzag through life. They get a good start on one thing, then are distracted to another, and off they go. They leave a trail of unfinished work, of goals that have been forgotten in the glamour of newer distractions. They are as confused as a four-year-old who tries to see everything going on in a three-ring circus.

August was a young Middle Western attorney, employed by a brass company. He was a butterfly. Butterflying made him take an extra year to complete his law course. He had intelligence enough, perhaps too much. He thought of too many things at the same time. He would drop the first to chase the second.

He thought so quickly that he kept getting off on other tracks. If he had had a slow, plodding, one-track mind, he would not have needed to learn to say "no" to himself.

It was a brilliant Bulgarian chemist, Dr. Stephen Popoff, who first called the merits of a one-track mind to my attention. Fascinated by chemistry, I was working overtime in the laboratory, starting one experiment before another was finished. I got hopelessly tangled up in them.

Dr. Popoff told me to carry a 2-cent pad, and, instead of trying out every notion that popped into my head, to make a brief note of it on the pad, meantime staying on the main track. That was in 1915. I have carried a pad ever since. Every evening I sort over the day's random notions that have occurred to me and been jotted down and file them away. The interesting thing is that, by nightfall, some of the bright ideas jotted down in the morning are filed most appropriately in the wastebasket.

That is an easy way of saying "no" to yourself.

August, the young corporation lawyer, tried the note-pad idea. It worked, and now he is never without one.

Saying "no" to yourself is not always that easy. There are parties, public meetings, social calls, movies.

I made it less necessary to say "no" to these distractions by moving to a tiny rural hamlet that turns time backward a century. The big city had too many enticing distractions for my good. About the only distractions I have now are suppers in country churches and long-distance telephone calls. In six months in a distraction-free environment I turn out more work than in a year in the city. Sure, I like city life and activity; that was the trouble, I liked it too well and my "no-power" was getting strained.

Say "no"—and mean it!—to the sidetracks.

Say "no" to the relishes and hors d'oeuvres so you will have more room for the roast. Don't be like the small boy who cried because he was so full of bread and jam that he couldn't eat the apple pie.

4. Use the obstacles for steppingstones

It's not difficult to stick to it when the going is easy. When the track is blocked, there is a strong temptation to take a permanent sidetrack. Leaders have found, however, that the obstacle can bring out more determination than ever and help them rise higher.

Kites fly highest against a stiff wind.

A young man, preparing for a shorthand contest, practiced diligently until he could write 300 words a minute. The night before the contest he went skating and had a bad fall. The following morning two fingers of his right hand were numb. They were broken!

There was a real obstacle. Did he quit the contest? If he had we would not know about him today. After the broken fingers had been set he tried holding a small potato in his injured hand while he wrote shorthand. Hurray! It worked.

He won the contest by making a steppingstone out of what might have seemed to be an obstacle.

I thought of him the other day when I stopped in Young's Gift Shop. A magnificently dressed woman came storming in with a puzzle she had bought the day before. She was mad.

"There is something wrong with this puzzle," she stormed. "I tried it for ten minutes and it wouldn't go together."

A small boy in the shop overheard her.

"Puzzle?" he asked, edging toward her. "Please may I look at it?"

He took it in his hands and had it put together in a jiffy.

"Imagine!" the woman exclaimed as she flounced out of the shop.

There are many women, however, who can show men that obstacles can be steppingstones. Bette Davis was a New England girl who wanted to become an actress. But an accident burned her around the eyes, which gave her a popeyed expression. Here was an obstacle, nearly a tragedy for a would-be actress.

Bette Davis made this burn into a steppingstone. She concentrated on training her eyes, to make them as expressive as possible. Audiences in the regular theaters sit too far back to see these expressive eyes, but movie talent scouts saw them.

Other actresses may have won Hollywood contracts because of their beautiful thighs. Bette Davis got her contract because of her expressive eyes. An accident that might have spelled tragedy had been made into a steppingstone.

Then there is Dotty Remy. She was a headline roller-skating artist at sixteen and had even performed for the King of England. Then something happened and she began to put on weight, more and more of it until she topped 200 pounds.

This might have been the end of her days as a star on skates. But, no, it was a steppingstone. She became a comedienne on skates.

Lydia O'Leary, as you might guess, was an Irish girl. She had a lot of Irish stick-to-itiveness, too. Her obstacle was a disfiguring birthmark, like a large squashed strawberry, right on her face. She made this her steppingstone. She devised a way to conceal such birthmarks from unkind stares of strangers. She now has her own flourishing factory, which makes Covermarks to help others change disfiguring obstacles into steppingstones.

As soon as Gracie was fifteen, the Fields family put her to work in a cotton mill, in Rochdale, England. The family needed her earnings. But Gracie found her job bloomin' dull. She sang above the whirr of the bobbins, to break the monotony of the work. She made up songs that were not very flattering to the foreman, but she and the other girls enjoyed them.

Her foreman was a blustery little chap. Gracie entertained the girls one afternoon with a burlesque imitation of their boss. Gracie thought it was funny and wondered why the girls did not laugh. Then she discovered that the boss had been standing behind her. That was the last entertaining she did in that factory.

Discouraged at being fired? Her conservative family thought it a disgrace, but they changed their attitude when her entertaining brought in $5,000 some weeks. Her "disgrace" was a steppingstone.

"I feel grateful to that foreman," Gracie Fields writes. "If he hadn't fired me I might be winding cotton in an English mill today, instead of winding around the world entertaining others.

"He taught me a lesson, too. *When a situation looks black don't take it for what it is on the surface.* Examine it in your mind, think it over. Is there a clue in that particular piece of bad luck which will lead you on to something better? Have the courage to ask yourself, 'What can I learn from this experience?' I learned and earned a lot by doing this very thing myself, and I wish you plenty of the same if you try it, too!"

Many others have found that bad luck is not what it usually seems on the surface. Instead of quitting, they change their grip, say "no," and convert the bad luck or obstacles into steppingstones.

Life began, not at forty, but at fifty, for a minister who had what many would have called bad luck. Physicians in Providence told him he must quit his work or his semi-invalid life might soon be at an end. There was an obstacle, for you know how much money a preacher might have saved to live on the rest of his life! But it was this very obstacle that gave the Reverend Wallace Nutting a new grip on life and led him to fame and fortune.

Deaf and half crippled, he turned to his hobby—photography. Propped up in bed, he colored prints of old New England houses and landscapes. His delicate colorings were unusual, and Wallace Nutting Platinum Prints became popular the country over. As his health gained he toured the country, taking photographs and writing books on the beauty of various states. The chances are that you have one of these books, or a framed platinum print, in your own home or perhaps a piece of furniture that was made in the factory he started for re-creating old furniture.

When you look at some of those nostalgic pictures of his, think of them now as visible evidence of stick-to-itiveness, of changing an obstacle into a steppingstone.

Skilled engineers sometimes find themselves out of jobs, through no fault of theirs. Sam Locke had studied at three famous engineering schools, but that didn't hold a job for him in the depression of 1930. He had to watch his expenditures, naturally, and bought some cheap coal, which was of such a low grade that it would not burn in his stove. But he could not afford to waste it.

Using his back yard as a laboratory, Sam Locke got an old oil barrel. He lined it with firebrick and old scraps of iron. He lit the fire, and the iron lining burned out, so he made some special firebricks and forgot the iron. At last he made a stove that would burn almost anything and that was remarkably efficient on fuel.

He still had no regular job, so he began making the stoves in his back yard. He sold them to neighbors for whatever price he could get. In 1937 he tried peddling the stoves and sold a total of thirty-five at prices ranging from $10 to $25. The next year he sold 200. In 1941 he sold 50,000 Locke stoves during the first eight months. The next year some 400,000 of the now famous Warm Morning heaters were sold.

When Sam Locke lost his regular job of $200 a month that was an obstacle for anyone, but in almost a decade he turned that obstacle into an income of more than $10,000 a month in royalties.

As some sage remarked, success is largely a matter of having nerve to stick to the ship when everybody else is jumping overboard.

The name Robert Dollar suggests steamship lines to most persons. It is true that Captain Dollar was in the steamship business, in a big way. Just a few years before the First World War he finally achieved the first world-wide steamship service under one flag and one owner-ship. He made a tremendous success operating ships, but it was an obstacle that he had changed into a stepping-stone, for he had been a woodsman.

His parents emigrated from Scotland, and before Robert was fourteen he was in the wilds of Canada, working as cook's boy in a remote lumber camp.

The cook's helper started work before sunup and was still cleaning up after sundown. There was just so much work to be done, and no regular hours to punch on a time clock. Dollar hurried through his work to get some spare time, and this nearly got him fired.

One afternoon Hi' Robinson, manager of the lumber camp, saw young Dollar sitting down. Loafing on the job, the manager assumed. But the lad explained that he was merely trying to overcome an obstacle.

"There's no school hereabouts, and I am trying to teach myself."

The manager did not fire him for loafing, but soon made the boy, who had yet to shave, temporary foreman of a group of logging men, men old enough to be his ancestors and rough as a fresh-mined diamond.

By the time Dollar was twenty-seven he had saved enough money to buy a small tract of timberland and go into business for himself. There came another obstacle, the panic ushered in by Black Friday. Dollar was wiped out, cleaned of every dollar he had, and in debt for a lot he didn't have.

He started over as a workman, cleaned up his debts, and bought another tract of timber, redwood this time. Then another obstacle came bounding his way—not a Wall Street panic this time, but inability to get a steamboat line to haul the timber from his tract. Probably I would have sold out for what I could get and started in on some safe, sure job then. But Robert Dollar was a better Scotsman than I am.

In a northern California port he located a wheezy little tub of a boat, the "Newsboy," which he could buy cheaply. An obstacle put Dollar into oceanic transportation. That 300-ton boat, with leaky seams, became the grand-daddy of the first world-wide fleet of ships. The obstacle of lack of transportation for his redwood logs became a steppingstone to the famous line of "President" liners, putting in as regularly as clockwork at all the principal ports on our globe.

When Cecil Rhodes was seventeen he ran head-on into an obstacle that was serious. His sickly nature broke and he had to fight his way back to health. Firm-lipped good-bys were said to his relatives in England, and he headed for the outposts of civilization in Africa, to regain his health and, incidentally, to transform his obstacle into a steppingstone, even into an empire. He developed diamond mines, smoothed the relations between the British and Dutch in South Africa, won the loyalty of kings of savage nations along the borders, laid the plans for a railway extending all the way from Capetown to Cairo, suppressed savage revolts, built telegraph lines and more railroads, became a hero in the Boer War.

That was the sickly lad whose health kept him from finding an opportunity in his homeland. Just thirty-two years of his life were spent in Africa, but on his death he left an empire and a fortune of more than thirty million dollars for others. And he died before he was fifty.

It is easy to take advantage of the good breaks. No leadership is required for that. The real leader can stick to it and make a profit from what might seem, at first, to be losses.

It is inevitable to have some bad breaks, sometime. A few errors of judgment are to be expected, also. But the leader recovers from these fumbles by sticking it out, not by running to the wailing wall.

When some general obstacle strikes all, such as a financial depression, a few firms have the leadership that converts the obstacle into a steppingstone. In the depression following the First World War, for instance, many firms came out stronger than before, because they had real leadership. Howard Heinz's father started in business peddling homemade horseradish. That was old H. J. Heinz, founder of the famous 57 Varieties.

Son Howard Heinz led the firm through the depression years of 1932 to 1935 by turning obstacles into step-pingstones. Other firms were cutting down, waiting for fair weather before going ahead. That made it easier for Heinz. Howard Heinz increased his advertising expenditures, introduced new products, brought out low-priced lines for the depression trade.

When the depression had blown over there was a great realignment of firms in the food field. Heinz had forged ahead while many of his competitors had permanently lost customers to him.

Fair-weather leaders are leaders in name only.

When others are jumping overboard, the real leader sticks to the ship.

Many of the obstacles that throw men for a loss are imaginary. Often the obstacles are nothing more serious than an ingrown alibi that the person comes to believe.

Ask yourself often, as I do: "Is it really an obstacle, or am I myself the obstacle?"

Usually the obstacle can be made a steppingstone.

The true leader thrives on obstacles. When everything runs smoothly he becomes homesick for some obstacle to overcome.

Success is most enjoyable when it has been won against odds.

5. *Pretend it is easy*

A psychologist in California gave some young folk a series of problems in arithmetic. Half the young people were told, "You will find these problems very difficult, but do the best you can, even though you may fail to solve many of them."

The other young people were told, "These are all

easy, but we still want you to work them, just for practice. You will probably get them all right, but let's work them anyway."

The children who approached the problems in expectation of failure did fail. They made more mistakes and took longer to work the problems than the other group.

It was not the problems that stumped the children; it was the spirit in which they went to work on the figures.

The attitude in which we approach a job makes all the difference in the world in our stick-to-itiveness and in our ultimate success.

One important factor in the unusual success of the National Cash Register Co. dates away back to its tiny beginnings. John Patterson, the founder, thought success, not failure. He taught success. He had every last man on the force thinking success.

An amazing number of our inventions have been made by men with no technical training in the field. They were outsiders, rank amateurs. But that was an advantage. They did not know that the thing they were tackling was considered impossible by the tradition-bound specialists.

A barber, for instance, invented the spinning frame.

A schoolteacher invented the cotton gin.

A janitor made the first microscope.

A coal miner invented the locomotive.

The telegraph was invented by a portrait painter.

A retail clerk invented automatic couplers for railroad cars.

A street contractor invented the sleeping car.

A textile man invented block signals to give railroads safety.

A schoolteacher gave us the electric locomotive.

And so it goes. They were just ignorant enough to think it would be easy, and easy did it. They didn't know enough to be discouraged.

That is what Charles F. Kettering had in mind when he said:

> *A man must have a certain amount of intelligent ignorance to get anywhere with progressive things.*

The Wizard of Menlo Park used intelligent ignorance. Thomas A. Edison paid no attention to theoretical difficulties. He would try something regardless of advice against it in books. He did not think about difficulties but hoped for results. "We will find it just around the corner" beckoned him on.

This is one reason why the real leaders and achievers have good streaks of optimism in their personalities. The optimism helps them see the easy side of things. They emphasize the easiness, not the difficulties.

During the California gold rush of '49 there was no quick transportation across the continent to the gold fields around Sacramento. A long trip by boat around the Horn was quicker than an overland trip. A boat trip to Panama, thence overland to the Pacific, was quicker. But this was a *rush*. A quicker way was needed.

Why not by boat to Nicaragua, up the rapids of the San Juan River by river steamer, to the continental divide? Just a few miles overland thence to the Pacific. That would save time and money.

So big, illiterate Cornelius Vander Bilt rushed river

boats to the Greytown lagoon, to inaugurate the overland short cut to California through Nicaragua.

The "S.S. Director" started upstream. Her crew and
the engineers spent a week trying to get her through the
three dangerous rapids. They returned. It was impossible
to navigate the rapids, they reported. It would tear the
bottom right out of the ship.

Big Connie fumed and cussed, and he was an artist at
both.

"Hell's delight," he howled. "What's skeerin' you
suckers! Try it and ye'll find it's easy. Come on, ye
skeeter smackers, I'll take the 'Director' up myself. Fust
ye get steam up, and then ye steam down. That's all thar
is to it. Git aboard now and we'll make it."

Through sand bars, alligators, fallen trees, and the
rocks and rapids, old Connie pushed the boat. They
made it.

"No, thar wasn't much to it," he said. "I jest tied down
the safety valve and jumped the damn rocks. The engineer fellers was skeered so they nigh puked. But we
made it. Hell, I knew all it needed was guts."

When you give instructions to someone, tell him it
will be easy.

When you tackle something yourself, pretend it will
be easy.

Don't lick yourself before you start.

Easy does it.

*"Lord, we do not ask thee for the desirable things of
life, but merely to tell us where they are and we will go
and get them."*—An old Scotch prayer.

For STICK-TO-ITIVENESS to GET
THINGS DONE

Sink your ships
Change your grip
Say "no" to yourself
Use obstacles for steppingstones
Pretend it is easy

13

How to use the most important hours of the day

There were several hundred supervisors and executives of war factories in the smoke-filled room in Providence. Their factories were booming. Most of them were smoking better cigars than usual.

They were at the meeting to get some help for their essential war plants, to learn how to keep up worker morale and factory production. And each of them had a personal problem, too.

"What will happen to us," they were thinking, "when we have to cut production? Many will be dropped from the pay roll. How can I be sure I will not be one?"

I mentioned this undercurrent of personal worry to my companion. He was an old man; born in poverty, he had educated and trained himself for industrial leadership. This was the second world war he had fought as a key leader in an essential factory. His white hair was thick and wavy, his face wrinkled, but ruddy, and his figure erect and lithe and his piercing blue eyes and smiling mouth radiated a friendly understanding. A stranger would have mistaken him for a college dean or president, not a factory man.

"What happens to them when the force is cut," he replied to my question, "all depends upon what they do with the most important hours of the day."

His glance fastened on a balding, tweedy man directly in front of us.

"Now consider Gene, here," he said. "He is now general manager of an important plant. He left school when he was sixteen to become a toolmaker's apprentice.

"Gene was a young supervisor under me in the First World War, in the plant at New Haven. He was the youngest supervisor we had and about the only one who was not an engineering graduate.

"The day the Armistice was signed in 1918 we closed down the plant. Everybody except a few old-timers was laid off.

"Then the directors thought we should try using some of our facilities for a different kind of manufacturing. None of us knew much about this new line. Frankly, we were afraid of it and suggested they get a new man to handle it. So their committee looked around a bit and found a man. Know who they found? Gene—and he wasn't much more than a kid.

"Seems he knew a little about the new line, and he was prepared to take charge of this development because he had been using the most important hours of the day."

I was puzzled.

"The most important hours of the day," I asked, "what are they?"

"The two hours at the end of the work day usually from five to seven o'clock," he continued. "Those are the hours when people taper off from their bread-and-butter work and decide what to do the rest of the day. In those two important hours some decide to go to a movie, play cards, go joy riding. Gene decided differently, and don't get the idea he was a prude; he can raise plenty of hell himself.

"In those important hours he asked some of the engineering professors at Yale to teach a squad of ambitious factory men, right in the professors' homes. Six nights a week he attended those informal classes. And his wife" —the older man chuckled at this—"she started attending, too; said it was the only time she could find to be with him.

"After he was put in charge of our new development, he taught similar classes for his subordinates, on his own time and initiative, right in his home, three nights a week. The other three nights he spent with a group, which he also organized, to learn some of the legal kinks of management from law professors.

"He gathered a bunch of inexperienced young fellows around him in the department—and we old-timers had been afraid to tackle the job. He made a success of it because he encouraged his men to use the most important hours of the day. During those hours, they made the right decisions about supervising themselves. Eight hours a day they bossed others, and they did not neglect to boss themselves in those two important hours after work.

"These men down there in the smoke of expensive cigars need not worry about what will happen to them in the big layoff, *if* they make the right decisions—to supervise themselves during those two important hours."

We continued to talk, the industrial sage and I, about others who had discovered that the gold of life, and security for the future, is won or lost in the decisions made during those hours just after work.

You have heard about some of them already, such as:

Henry Ford worked evenings on his own time to develop his car.

George Eastman did likewise with his new dry plates.

Alexander Graham Bell worked on his telephone during those hours.

You may not have heard about a telephone research engineer, however, who decided, between five and seven o'clock, to experiment with the chemistry of vitamins— something not at all related to the telephone. He improvised a home laboratory, and was the first to discover, in 1936, how to make vitamin B_1. Tons and tons of this vitamin are made each year, under the patents that a decision about using his hours after work brought to telephone researcher R. R. Williams.

We owe modern radio and electronics to a man employed by Western Electric, who developed the detector and other radio tubes on his own, after hours. That was Lee De Forest.

Nathaniel Hawthorne became a leading author of his day, not because he worked a full day all week long as clerk in the customs house, but because he decided between five and seven o'clock to write his immortal stories.

And before Hawthorne, an employee of the British War Office, Thomas Macaulay, became a leading writer by making the right decisions between five and seven o'clock.

Don't overlook Albert, either. His father had a small electrical business that "took a turn for the worse." Another reverse came to the boy in school. The courses were mostly languages, which he did not like and in which he made a miserable record. But he got hold of a worn-out geometry book and read it evenings, teaching himself the mathematics he could not get at school.

He failed the entrance examinations for engineering college. In a few years he had a small job as examiner in the Patent Office. All the while he was investing his evenings in teaching himself higher mathematics and using his spare moments in the Patent Office for trying out new mathematical twists. When he was only twenty-six Albert Einstein published five papers of his mathematical discoveries, including a "Special Theory of Relativity." It was not his job or his school courses that made this possible; it was the right decisions in the most important hours of the day.

It is almost impossible, in fact, to find a leader in any field who has not made the right decisions for self-management during those two vital hours.

Marcus H. Brown left school after the sixth grade. After trying many jobs he finally ended up as truck driver for the famous observatory on Mount Wilson. That was a good steady, year-around job. But as Marcus was driving loads of astronomers and visitors up and down the mountain he did some thinking and decided to manage himself. He figured he would find out all about telescopes by making one himself, from start to finish.

He got an armful of books and learned how to grind a lens. He procured an old truck, which he used as power to turn his grinding wheels. The other drivers laughed at him, chided him for neglecting their pinochle games. But Marcus borrowed still more books from the library, learned more about telescopes.

Then it was announced that $6,000,000 of Rockefeller funds were being given Mount Wilson to erect the world's greatest telescope.

And the chap the other truck drivers had called "nuts" was given the job of supervising the grinding of the giant 200-inch mirror for this new telescope.

The optician in charge, Marcus H. Brown, made the right decisions between five and seven o'clock. The boys who thought he was foolish are still driving their trucks.

There is ample precedent for Marcus H. Brown. Shortly before the Revolutionary War William Herschel was making a fair enough living as church organist and giving private music lessons. He was an immigrant who had left his native Hanover and his nine brothers and sisters for the greater opportunities in England. When he was twenty-five he made some decisions for himself and began to use every minute of his spare time between lessons and church services to study. He taught himself higher mathematics, optics, and astronomy. The things he read about he tried out, starting with a big tin telescope he made himself.

In fifteen years people began to hear about William Herschel and the homemade telescopes with which he had been viewing the heavens most of the night. He was no longer the humble German youth with the funny accent; he was the man who had discovered the planet Uranus. On the heels of this he discovered two satellites of Saturn and two of Uranus. He was the first to observe the periodical nature of sunspots. Twenty-five hundred new nebulae and star clusters were discovered by this organist who was appointed the Royal Astronomer. His living was comfortable enough as organist and music teacher, but he became Sir William Herschel by knowing how to use the most important hours of the day.

Two thousand years ago Plutarch wrote this:

"One day, over their cups, Philip of Macedon, with a kind of sneer, introduced some discourse about the odes and tragedies which Dionysius the Elder had written, and pretended to doubt how he could find the time for such works. Dionysius, the son, answered smartly enough, 'They were written in the time which you and I, and other happy fellows, spend over the bowl.'"

After the industrial sage told me the story of Gene and the most important hours of the day, I removed the glass from my watch and marked the entire sector from five to seven o'clock in bright red lacquer.

This red warns me several times daily that the decisions I make for myself during those relaxing hours may be the most critical decisions of the day.

Leaders advance themselves.

Failures have pleasant dreams of their future; successes have clear visions of their future.

14

Getting power over time

This is a story of a worried soldier, a glittering blonde, a breathless politician, and the Salvation Army. Each of these tells a valuable story for leadership.

The hour-and-a-quarter wait between trains had not appealed to me, even though I was to wait in the large new station in the state capital. I accepted it as one of the unavoidable evils of going around the country talking on leadership. Like a good traveler, I'd make the best of it, little realizing the experience in store for me.

I read the morning paper with more care than usual, to use up as much time as possible. That done, I took some postal cards from my pocket and brought my correspondence up to date.

A group of some thirty young men, in double column, marched raggedly past, selectees on their way to an army camp. I silently wished them courage and strength.

A down-and-outer, red face bloated, asked for my newspaper and quickly disappeared before the police officer turned around.

I watched a little old lady, who had apparently mislaid her ticket, search frantically for it.

A deputy sheriff came in, handcuffed to a well-dressed, middle-aged man, on his way to the state penitentiary. The prisoner, smoking incessantly, kept pulling down his sleeve to try to conceal the handcuff.

A worried-looking soldier appraised me carefully, then came up and sat beside me. "Say, doc," he whispered, "can you do a favor for a feller who has had some bad luck?"

He was due back at camp at noon, he said, but had missed his train and would be hours over leave. I could help him out of his bad luck, he urged, if I'd be a good sport and write a letter for the military police, just to say that he was in my office getting treatment for a sick spell when the train left.

I was sorry that my whiskers had misled him. My specialty is the treatment of people who need to improve the way they manage others and themselves. Apparently he needed a lot of help on that, especially on managing himself. Just how did he happen to miss the train, anyway? But the soldier did not want to talk about such theoretical things and shuffled over to the Red Cross booth, where he ate a few sandwiches, then to the station master, who finally wrote something on a piece of paper for him.

While pondering the soldier's predicament, and his unsoldierly solution of it, I heard a commotion at the large south entrance. A score of Salvation Army folk was entering. They were laughing boisterously. Several of them carried small children in their arms. Others carried toys for the children. Two of the adults carried baggage.

This joyful band, none of whom received more than $20 a week pay, took possession of two long facing benches. The children were set on the floor to play. One man passed around a bag of bananas. It was as much fun as a family picnic. Eyes were bright, cheeks flushed, voices happy.

It was a solemn occasion in a way, however, for they were at the station to bid Godspeed to two members who were being transferred to work overseas in battle zones.

They had arrived a full half hour before the streamliner express would depart. It was a happy, short half hour. Watching them made it that way for me, too.

There was a sudden bustle of activity when the train caller announced the arrival of the streamliner. In a few minutes the station was empty. Nothing can be emptier than a quiet railroad station, I thought. I was still smiling about the antics of the Salvation Army babies on the floor, as I settled back to finish my correspondence.

Suddenly the south entrance swung open. A dazzling blonde, in rich fur coat, came running in. Two hotel porters were loaded down with her baggage. I wondered if she were a society bud or a night-club entertainer. I wondered if she would make the train and if she had needed to be late.

The gatetender stopped her. All seats on the streamliner were reserved, and she had no ticket. She rushed to the ticket window, but no seats were left.

Her voice echoed in the cavernous quiet of the empty station as she told the man at the ticket window what she thought about the way he ran the railroad. Then I knew she was a night-club entertainer.

The echo of her profane remarks had scarcely died down when the entrance swung open again, and a very fat policeman dashed in. He was holding his hat with one hand. He was short of breath already, and his feet slipped on the polished floor.

The gatetender opened the gate and the policeman ran up the stairs into the train shed without slowing down. Another officer came running in, at a dog trot, supporting on his arm a tall, elderly, richly dressed man who was pale and breathless. I recognized the tall man as a well-known political figure in the state. He, too, was late for the streamliner but was counting on the power of the law to hold it for him.

The excitement of this race against time was more than I could take sitting down. I walked rapidly to the gate, to see if he did catch the train.

"Funny, isn't it," the gatetender volunteered, "the way people wait until the last minute, and then blame us. The old coot will be lucky if he makes it, but those folk from the Salvation Army will have a pleasant trip, won't they?"

I loitered at the gate a few minutes. Then the fat policeman returned, hat in hand and wiping perspiration from his brow.

"Did he make it?" I asked, with the eager curiosity of a man who watched the start of a race.

"Naw!" the officer replied, leaning against the hand-rail to catch his breath. "The old so-and-so didn't have his ticket, even if he had caught the train. Anyway, as soon as he got upstairs he couldn't take so much running and passed out, cold! I nearly did myself."

The policeman put his hat back on and pulled away from the railing.

"And the old sport had nothing to do all morning except catch this train," he blew up. "Why did they ever

pick on me to look after him? What he needs is a gov-
erness. Now I gotta get the ambulance. Whew!"

In the papers the next morning I read a brief item that
Mr. Politician had had a sudden heart attack in the railroad station at the state capital and that physicians pro-
nounced him out of danger.

I believe the physicians were wrong. The politician
will always be in danger, the danger that lurks in every
fleeting minute of the day for those folk who wait until
the last minute. He was a powerful politician but lacked
power where it is more important—power over himself,
which the real leader uses to give him power over time.

Use time; remember you are not going to live forever.

And recall Cecil Rhodes' dying words: "So little
done, so much left to do!"

In his early printing shop, Benjamin Franklin also sold
stationery and books. A traveler picked out a book one
afternoon and asked the clerk in the front office its
price.

"That is $1.25."

"But I think it should be less," said the traveler. "Ask
the proprietor if he will not give me a better price. You
have had this book for several years without selling it."

Franklin was called in from the back room, face and
hands stained with ink. The clerk explained that the
customer wanted the book cheaper.

"Why, that book is worth $1.40," Franklin said.

"What! Your clerk said it was only $1.25."

"That *was* the price. It is worth more now, for you
have taken 15 cents' worth of my time."

The self-made president of a large electrical manufacturing firm keeps his office clock and his watch five

minutes fast. Visitors occasionally call this apparent error to his attention.

"Since I have been eighteen," the chief answers, "my watches and clocks have always been that way. By being only five minutes ahead of the other fellow I have a great advantage. The man who is late starts off with two strikes on him. He has to hurry and cannot be thorough. He has to apologize and thus weakens his leadership. He makes someone irritable and that loses cooperation. I don't let a clock run me. I keep ahead of the clock."

There is one natural resource we all share equally—time. It cannot be hoarded. We get our full share only by using it as it slips by.

The opposite page is printed so that it may be removed from the book and framed or slipped under the glass on your desk top.

CPSIA information can be obtained at www.ICGtesting.com
Printed in the USA
BVOW06s0003270416

445447BV00024B/92/P